MONEY, YOU CAN HACK IT

101 Creative Ways To Increase Your Net Worth,
Grow Your Wealth, and Have Fun Along The Way

Frankie Calkins

Foreword by John Chapman

www.TheMoneyResolution.com
frankie@themoneyresolution.com

Follow The Money Resolution on YouTube for personal finance videos weekly!

#MYCHIBOOK

Dedication

For Tucker & Leo

Who taught me that attitude (& patience) are everything 🐾

A SPECIAL GIFT FOR YOU

MONEY, YOU CAN HACK IT
Bonuses & Companion Guide

You Get:
10 Bonus Hacks
Downloadable 101 Hacks Checklist
Alternate book cover designs
A complete list of all recommended resources
Frankie's annual budget spreadsheet
Ongoing updates about future projects
And more!

Claim your free gift at:
www.TheMoneyResolution.com/HackIt

TABLE OF CONTENTS

Foreword

Starting from scratch. Boy, that would be nice.

How much did Frankie start with?

NEGATIVE $85,000.

As in, his net worth was negative $85,000. When I say net worth, I mean all of his money, minus all of his debts, was in the red. Not exactly something you see people talking about on social media...

Was it just laziness? Because, you know, some people just "don't put in the work."

Or maybe it was a lack of smarts.

Wrong. And WRONG.

Frankie is a graduate from the University of Washington - one of the top public universities in the country.

Oh, and after graduating, he joined Teach for America (which is known for not taking on any old slouch) and went on to work in education for 5 years before jumping into marketing full time.

The problem was, even with his hard work ethic and smarts, Frankie had yet to master his finances.

So after almost a decade of full-time work after college, the shoe dropped.

It all started with an in-depth goal-setting session where he wrote out his SMART goals and....

Just kidding. That never happened. I'd hardly even call his initial endeavor a goal since it was just a shift in perspective.

It was as if he said, "NO, I will no longer have a negative net worth..." And "No, I don't expect anyone to do this for me..." And "heck YES, I'm going to pursue this personal finance thing."

So, in 2018, like a swimmer diving into the Arctic Ocean during the polar bear plunge, his journey began!

What's amazing is - in just 1 ½ years, Frankie went from $85k in debt, to #NetWorthZero, without winning the lottery, getting money from family, or striking gold in the backyard.

Curious to hear how he did it?

In his first book, *The Money Resolution: 101 Ways To Save Money, Make Money, and Get Out of Debt In One Year*, Frankie offers an up-close and personal look at how his life transformed in a year, and 101 ways you can change yours.

But that was only the beginning.

Frankie even admits that part of the problem of writing this book was that he found he had TOO much to write about. His momentum is building. And in this book, you can feel that he's only getting started!

What you are about to embark on is a book with 101 MORE personal finance tips. This time, he focused on how to increase your net worth, grow your wealth, and have fun along the way.

Wait, did he say fun?

Um, yeah. Actually, having read the book, one of the best parts of it is that Frankie presents money hacks in a way that feels... enjoyable.

As Frankie states, though, it's easier to describe what a hack is NOT, rather than what it IS.

Hacks aren't about guarantees or schemes. Hacks are real, tangible, and actionable. Best of all, hacks are powerful.

A few of my favorite personal hacks in the book include:

- #17 The Starve and Stack Method
- #20 The Can I Afford 5 Rule
- #66 Take a Money Health Day
- #89 Achieve a F.I. Alternative
- #93 Pay Off Your Student Loans Through Work

It's one thing to have an answer to a problem. I mean, you could search online and find an answer to a question in a millisecond.

But it's another to feel capable of executing on a problem and excited to take action.

A word of caution: Don't consume this like a textbook. It's meant to be consumed in bite size chunks, helping to spur new ideas and look at old topics in new ways. It's meant to be carried with you on your kindle, or sit at your bedside so you can keep coming back to it often.

Have you felt overwhelmed by the topic of money? Maybe you're not sure who to talk with or feel scared to ask a dumb question.

Or maybe you've run into some roadblocks before and aren't sure how to break on through.

I can assure you that what you hold in your hands is a very special treat. Frankie has poured his heart into it, capturing so many useful hacks and distilling them in a creative way for you to read. Heck, these are hacks he's used! Proof that they can be powerful.

You'll walk away feeling educated and, more importantly, empowered to take action.

Be free. Financially, that is.

John Chapman, Host of The John Chapman Show

Introduction

"To act is to modify the shape of the world"
-Jean-Paul Sartre

I was writing an entirely different book. As I sat staring at my completed outline and well-researched notes my eyes drifted to Chapter 7: Taxes. Then Chapter 8: Mutual Funds & ETFs. *Riveting stuff* I thought to myself. I've become a self-proclaimed personal finance nerd and even I was bored with those topics. I started to reflect on my first book "The Money Resolution" and wondered, *What was it people liked most about that one?* and *What did I enjoy most about writing it?*

One reviewer on Amazon liked the bit about claiming free money owed to you using a website I shared. A friend of mine told me she didn't realize you could invest money in your Health Savings Account (HSA). A family member and mortgage broker once explained he learned a thing about student loan forgiveness after watching one of my YouTube videos. Others have brought up learning about Roth IRAs, Acorns, side hustle ideas, and how to ask for a raise and why you should. Then it hit me. People naturally drift to new ideas they can relate to—creative ideas that are genuinely useful. Even better if they're actionable ideas that most people don't know about. New. Relatable. Actionable. Useful. Creative. It makes total sense! So I wondered, *can I write an entire book filled with these types of actionable ideas? If hacks are fun and money is boring, can I try to make money fun with hacks?*

As much as it pained me, I scrapped everything I had written and decided to try this new direction for the book. Sometimes the best ideas are the simplest and often your best work is created when passion strikes. I got right to work. What you hold in your hands (or digital screens) is that pivot, one year later: my favorite, most useful, most actionable, most up-to-date, most creative money hacks. Plus, dad jokes, puppies, and personal stories of success and failures, of course.

Why do I believe in hacking so much? The truth is, I believe hacking is powerful because it makes you feel as if you know something someone else doesn't. It's a leg up. A unique idea. An advantage. After some reflection, I realized I have always loved life hacking. A few examples:

- When I was a kid, I was obsessed with video games but hated losing or wasting time (this holds true). When I learned about warp whistles in Mario Bros. 3, my eyes opened. My brother even invited his teenage friends over to watch his 5-year-old brother beat the game in one sitting.
- In college, before portable Bluetooth speakers were a thing, I discovered that cell phone speakers sounded better when you could bounce the sound off of a larger surface. I created a cardboard-toilet-paper-roll-iPhone-speaker-amplifier-thing and presto! Jack Johnson and Incubus were practically in the dorm room performing live.
- I'm an avid year-round iced coffee drinker and recently came across a hack to freeze coffee to use as ice cubes in your coffee. This way, your iced coffee never gets watered down, especially during hot months (so, only July and August in Seattle...). Genius!

But I digress...

So what is money hacking and why should it matter to you? First, let's start with what money hacking is not:

It is not a guaranteed shortcut to success. It is not a silver bullet. It is not a get-rich-quick scheme. What someone else describes as a money hack might come off as obvious or completely unusable because hacking is not universal. Hacks cannot be universally applied to individual lives and individual situations.

Describing what money hacks are is far more difficult than telling you what they are not. But this brings up a critical point: hacking money requires looking at personal finance through a new, creative lens. It's taking action and experimenting. It's failing. It's learning. It's trying again, succeeding, and attempting to replicate that success. I can tell you from experience, stumbling upon a life or money hack that works wonders for you feels like a cheat code from video games. It's as if you know a secret nobody understands. And let me tell you... it's addictive. For me, it's also nostalgic.

Do you remember collecting change in a jar when you were young? And walking to the bank to ask for change roll wrappers? And running home to crack open that jar to sort and stack and count your way to riches? Completing a roll of pennies and holding it in your hand felt like a bar of gold. Plus, now you could buy *anything*! Fun Dip! Pogs! Big League Chew!

Where has this feeling gone? We weren't scared of change. We loved collecting it, counting it, and protecting it like it was a living, breathing pet we had to care for. How can we get this feeling back as grown ups? It's actually pretty simple. Let's hack it. Let's turn money into a game again. Let's make earning, saving, and spending fun. We don't need to be scared of taxes, rising interest rates, international trade tariffs, and more we don't care to fully understand. Instead, let's figure out how to watch our money grow in ways we didn't realize were possible. Let's get creative with money.

There's one small catch to consider before we get started: money is much less tangible these days. Many people rarely carry cash of any kind. Our money is essentially a string of zeros and ones in a matrix we can't physically touch. Our wallets are in our phones and bartering is hardly a thing. That's what makes getting good with money easy to ignore. *Out of sight, out of mind.* It's a convenient excuse, I'll admit.

Why should you prioritize collecting something you can't see and touch? Why does personal finance feel less personal and *way* too complicated? How can we succeed in a world that sometimes feels designed to take instead of give? Those are fair questions. But too often we give up before we give ourselves a chance to succeed.

The good news is there are a gazillion resources available to us. People. Books. Apps. And yes, even that jar full of change on your dresser. It's difficult to keep up with the best strategies, legislation, and tools to help you succeed. But it's not difficult to spend a few minutes a day trying something new to develop financial creativity. That's what this book is all about.

In my steady march towards #NetWorthZero, I tried every idea I discovered or came up with. I changed my net worth by six-figures in less than two years. I'm *finally* worth *something* and I can't wait to share all the fun ways I did it and the resources I recommend. I can't wait for you to feel what it's like to discover the immense power of financial literacy, to earn compound interest, and to develop momentum towards your financial goals. And so... I present this book and the following chapters as your **up-to-date, no-nonsense, actionable, creative compilation of tips to make money <u>fun</u> with hacks so you can improve your net worth and develop good money habits that stick.**

I've done my best to weed out the obvious and to avoid repeat ideas from "The Money Resolution". Once again, I've included a checklist at the end of the book to help you stay organized and return to your favorite ideas that encourage you to take action.

Of course, hacking won't solve all of your problems. While we're at it, *money* won't solve all of your problems. But hacking money can help you get a handle on your financial outlook Money hacks help you find your own answers and useful methods, as long as you have to have an open mind and personal goals. With that said, I have four goals for you, the reader:

1. Help you identify your why
2. Help you identify how much is enough
3. Provide you with unique and creative personal finance knowledge, tips and skills to help you get to your enough
4. Help you discover and develop your financial superpower

I encourage you to keep track of how you feel as you go through this book. What are you learning? Are these hacks sustainable and what are the trade-offs? Track your biggest money hurdles and roadblocks. Track what works for you and think about how to amplify those successes. But most importantly, don't give up. You could try 10 of these hacks and feel unsuccessful. But one hack and win later, you might discover your financial game changer.

But that's not my goal or guarantee. I simply hope this book helps you think more creatively about your money. I hope it helps you improve your life a little bit today, a little bit more tomorrow, and exponentially more in the days and years that follow. I hope you'll feel inspired to tackle your financial struggles head-on by taking consistent action. I hope you'll learn to believe in yourself and remain positive and grateful. And I want you to *have fun* doing it.

Let's begin with the first unofficial hack. It's simple but essential:

Forgive Yourself.

Stop beating yourself up for mistakes you've made or procrastination that has delayed your success. You won't be able to focus on the future if you spend energy thinking about the past. Embrace your debt and the choices that got you there. We all have room for improvement. Start fresh, think forward, and stay positive. Mindset is everything. Now, let's get started!

PART 1

Foundational Money Hacks

CHAPTER ONE

Productivity Hacks

"You do not rise to the level of your goals.
You fall to the level of your systems."
-James Clear

A curve-ball already? I bet you didn't expect we'd spend the first chapter NOT addressing money directly. The truth of the matter is, our goals are meaningless without systems. Consider this: every day you're either getting closer to your goals OR you're taking a step back. And remember, taking just one step back means you have to take TWO steps to move forward. That's a lot of pressure to put on yourself. This is where creative hacks come into play.

Perhaps you've heard these common productivity hacks: Listen to music. Or turn it off. Get a standing desk. Or try sitting. Eat a healthy breakfast. Skip breakfast. Eat a huge, unhealthy breakfast. Go to the gym in the morning. Afternoon. No, night time so you'll fall asleep quicker and get more rest. Set your alarm for 5 AM. Or let your body tell you when to wake up. Meditate during lunch. Work 20 minutes on, 5 minutes off throughout the day... You get the point. Hacks are meant to shake up your routine and get you to try something new that you haven't thought of before.

In researching this chapter I found and tried it all. And the truth is, depending on the day of the week, time of day, my current to-do list, and heck, even the weather, I had varying degrees of success. But net net, I was FAR more productive. I shook up how I tackled sections and chapters of this book by leveraging new software and spending a few hours writing every Saturday and Sunday. I took supplements. I went to the gym and ran outside, like a lot. Sometimes I spent more time finding and trying new methods to be more productive than... well, working if I'm being honest. But in my experimenting to find the perfect productivity hacks, I became smarter with my time and gained knowledge about what works for me—body and brain.

Speaking of the brain, let's start with your money mentality...

1. YOU NEED A WHY

"A resolution is basically just a wish list"
-Tony Robbins

I hate to lead with such a heavy topic for the first hack, but here's a truth I've learned about myself: if I don't know why I'm doing something, it's hard for me to do it well. Perhaps that sounds familiar to you...

"Start With Why" by Simon Sinek is one of the most impactful books I've read in the last year. It helped me adjust my thinking about, well, everything. Deep down, we all know what we *should* be doing—as in, we all know the difference between right and wrong. We all set goals and have motivations. But, how often do we really stop and think about our big picture *whys*?

If you picked up this book, you're serious about getting your financial life together. Either that or you were looking for some quick financial wins. And if that's the case, this is not what you were expecting. Deep philosophical reflecting? You bet. Because money is 90% psychological and only 10% mathematical. The *why* question sounds simple but sometimes the simplest questions can help us discover our most profound desires and answers. Without understanding your why, you may miss the point of this book and these suggestions entirely.

And so I ask you... if you want to get good with money, WHY? Take a moment and actually think about it. What would it mean? What are your goals? How much is enough? What are you willing to do to get there? No, no. Not, crime. Stay focused. Are you trying to help someone besides yourself? Are you in a hole of debt you're looking to climb out of? Are you looking to change your life and think money alone will do that? Let me act like a child and continue to ask: Why?

The typical answer is: So I can be less stressed.

But the truth is, money can help you picture a completely different future. Money can help you pursue a passion. Money can help you care for your family. Money can help you give and make an impact on the world. Money is freedom. And education about money is the fastest path to freedom. To learn is why you picked up this book. But your deep down *why* is up to you to discover.

You see, money is simply a tool, an incredibly powerful tool when you learn how to successfully wield it. It can help you get where you want to go. So where do you want to go? I challenge you to think beyond solving any immediate, specific problems like a looming bill. Getting good with money, as a skill, can actually change your life. But only if you know your why. Contrary to popular belief:

You don't need a budget. You need a why.

Your why is not a goal. Whys are far different. Whys are the reasons you set goals. It would be worthless to set a goal without understanding the deep down logic, reasoning, and emotion behind it. This is the part where I'm going to ask you to dig deep. You've picked up this book. You've made a decision to learn about money and find ways to improve your situation. Why? The challenge is this: in 3 words, express your why.

Your three words could be three reasons. Your three words could be a phase. They could be names. They could be feelings. Your three words could be anything. Next, take time to write more about your why. Spend some time digging into it and challenging your thought process. Fight with it. Hug it. Own it. Share it.

My three words that express my why are FREEDOM, TIME, and EDUCATION:

- **Freedom**: The ability to do what I want, when I want. The ability to discover a passion and follow it. The ability to work for myself and set my own schedule. It's relaxing on a deck by the water in the morning with a good book and playlist, one day. It's working 12 hours the next day on a project I'm obsessed with. It's the opposite of anxiety.
- **Time**: Time to spend with loved ones. Time to continue creating and doing what I love. Time is our most valuable asset. It's a finite, limited resource that we'll never get back. I'd like to make the most of it by worrying less and enjoying life more.
- **Education**: The knowledge I need to give myself power and control over my life. Knowing how to help myself, and ultimately knowing enough to help others after that. I want to be a lifetime learner and lifetime educator.

Money isn't happiness, but money provides freedom, and freedom can lead to happiness. Freedom to follow your passions. Freedom to take time and travel. Freedom to donate your time or money to the things you care about. And I've learned this: you can live rich and feel free without being wealthy. For me, my money journey shifted in one year. For you, it might be 6 weeks or it might be 6 years. That's okay. Enjoy the journey. The light flickers and the tunnel brightens with every meaningful, creative step you take. Follow your north star. Follow your why.

Read next: "Start With Why" by Simon Sinek

2. THE "JUST ONE THING" RULE

Each day, set out to accomplish *just one thing*. Most days, I create a to-do list (more on my love of lists in a moment) and when I'm done, I review and put a star next to my "just one thing". If I get nothing else done today, I *must* do at least this one thing.

As previously mentioned, every day you're either getting closer to your goals OR you're taking a step back. Admittedly, this is a bit of an extreme mindset but it motivates me. I want to get better in many areas of my life every single day but to make that less overwhelming, I focus on the one task I must complete today. This makes it much easier to chunk huge projects (like writing a book) into small tasks that I can tackle one day at a time.

It can be overwhelming to try to do everything at once. Instead, one giant check mark each day can really add up, especially if you focus on your finances often as your "just one thing". Not sure where to start?

- Try a hack from this book.
- Automate a bill or savings contribution.
- Pay back a friend for your half of the pizza from last weekend.
- Open up a Roth IRA and invest in that mutual fund you've been considering.

Just do one thing. Something. Anything.

When I feel stuck, I recreate my list. Typically my "just one thing" ends up being the first thing I write down. I can't tell you how many lists I have in my notebook with just one or two boxes out of 10 checked off. What's fun is finding a two-week-old list and realizing I can now cross off every damn thing.

I like to take the "Just One Thing" Rule and tack on the "1% A Day Rule" when I'm feeling extra ambitious. Which is usually. After I've done my "just one thing", I go even further by trying to get 1% better each day with my project or task. For example, with every YouTube video I make, I try one new thing to improve them. Each time I lead a meeting at work, I try to find a way to make it more engaging and efficient. Over time, these small improvements add up and make a huge difference so that I'm not only accomplishing more, I'm accomplishing more... better. Incremental improvement goes a long way over time!

Now, take these rules and apply them to your money. Tackling one money task a day is a great start, but not if all you do is log into your accounts and obsess over how they look. Ideally, you'll start spending this time with actionable items like reading (look at you now!), trying out a new personal finance podcast (recommendations in Chapter 17), watching educational videos, goal-setting (see the "25/5 Rule" in Chapter 13), and focusing on reducing your biggest expenses (see Section 2 for help with this).

Now, let's talk more about the power of lists...

3. CREATE LISTS

I love lists. You'll notice many throughout this book and on my YouTube channel. I recreate my to-do list for work at least once a day —either to start my morning or to end my workday and prepare myself for the day ahead. When I applied this to-do list strategy to my money, I found it to be a game-changer. Here are some list exercises (in list form!) that could help you tackle your finances more productively so you can become a powerful list-making Jedi:

Create a "Now, This Week, Some Day List"
NOW are things you'd like to tackle today. THIS WEEK are, as you'd expect, the things you'd like to accomplish within a week. SOMEDAY is the key. The point of this list is to declutter and focus on priorities. Putting to-do's in the SOMEDAY list gives yourself permission to let future tasks live in the future and focus on the most urgent priorities.

Start a "Ta-Da List"
This list is all about celebrating what you have gotten done. As I described in my book "The Money Resolution", I tracked my money accomplishments (and struggles...) in a note in my phone throughout the year. Come December, I reflected back on my wins and realized that these notes were essentially the outline for a book. Writing a book might not be your goal, but seeing your ta-da list grow can give you a sense of accomplishment and momentum.

Use a Bullet Journal to track your money and goals.
Some swear by crafting their own Excel spreadsheets or using online

tools like YNAB (You Need A Budget). For others, myself included, good ol' pen and paper is most effective. My favorite method is using a bullet journal, a notebook with tiny dots instead of lines, because it's completely customizable. You can set and track goals, write to-do lists, keep a budget, and manage all things finance in one place. To get started, outline what you want to track and section it off with a table of contents using hand-written page numbers. Here are a few more ideas for your journal: document bills, track spending, plan debt payoff, monitor savings, map out your money hack-tion items! Lists inside lists inside lists… a dream come true!

Read on: The Penny Hoarder "6 Simple Ways to Use a Bullet Journal to Manage Your Money"

4. DEDICATE 5 MINUTES A DAY

I have an app on my phone called "7 Minute Workout". The idea is that you can get fit if you dedicate just 7 minutes a day to exercise. When I started my fitness journey, I didn't have a gym membership so I gave this a shot at home. And you know what, it worked! It was a hassle to get in a rhythm at first, but just 7 minutes? I had no excuse to avoid it.

I LOVE the idea of applying this to personal finance. Like losing weight, getting your financial life in order can sound like a monumental task. I get it. It's much easier to avoid it than work on it for hours. However, if you build in a daily 5-minute habit, you'll have no excuse to avoid your finances. This is how we build muscle memory and habits. Sound easy enough? Great, it is! But what does it look like in practice? Well, here's what it doesn't look like:

- Logging in to your bank and obsessing over your accounts
- Looking at your credit score daily
- Bragging on social media about how much money you made side hustling last week
- Clicking on a YouTube ad about how to get rich quick

- Anything related to pyramid schemes...

Here's what it should look like:

- Checking your credit card balances every few days and making regular payments to keep your balances at zero
- Staying on top of your net worth and/or credit score once a week or bi-weekly
- Updating your spreadsheet with yesterday's spending (if you're a budget-er)
- Requesting money on Venmo from that friend that keeps promising to pay you back
- Transferring money to your high-interest online savings account to earn better than the almost 0% interest at big banks
- Paying a bill and looking into ways to reduce said bill in the future
- Calling to ask for better rates for insurances or lower interest on your credit card
- Listening to a podcast, reading a blog post, watching a YouTube video, or reading a chapter of a book on personal finance (check!)

If you haven't figured it out by now, I am a big fan of small efforts, day in and day out. Like compound interest, a little effort every day can really add up.

I learned recently that on average, people that participate in fantasy football spend just under 8 hours a week on their team. Even if this isn't you, this example shows most of us can find 35 minutes a week to put towards our finances!

Don't become obsessed, become educated. Become consistent. Become mission-driven and take action. I quoted Robert Collier, author of self-help books in the early 1900, in my first book "The Money Resolution" and it feels valuable to repeat it again: "Success is the sum of small efforts, repeated day in and day out." Similarly, he also said, "Constant repetition carries conviction." I'd tattoo it on my body if tattoos weren't so expensive...

> **Pro Tip**: If every day isn't realistic, I recommend "the two-day rule." Give yourself the ability to miss one day here and there. But don't allow yourself to go for two days consecutively without working on yourself and your money.

5. USE YOUR NEW SECRET WEAPON: THE WEEKEND

Raise your hand if this sounds like you: *I work hard all week and live for the weekend.*

I'll admit, that used to be me. I'm not going to argue that you should add an 8 hour side-hustle every Saturday and Sunday. The human body needs mental and physical breaks and plenty of sleep, especially to recover after a long work-week. The mind needs rest. The soul needs... fun! However, if you want to earn extra income, start a project, work on your finances, read a book, take money-hack action, and level-up your financial life... look no further than the weekend.

In a practical sense, your body operates best when it gets into a regular sleep rhythm. Therefore, going to bed and waking up at *similar* hours to your 9-5 during the weekend can help you stay on top of your productivity game. So, instead of sleeping in, see what you can get done in the early hours on the weekend. Start with 20 minutes one day. Up it to one hour. Then one hour both mornings. Even as a night owl, feeling productive on the weekend mornings (whether projects, working out, meal planning or more) was a true game-changer for me. It helped me sleep better throughout the week and also avoid the Sunday scaries.

With time, you might just find this extra weekend productivity spilling into your workweek, too. I see writing and creating YouTube videos as my 5-9 and often find myself getting up early before my day job so I can dive into project metrics and plan out my work-after-work agenda to be most effective with my personal time. Sound overwhelming? Start with just 5 minutes a day.

6. MAKE A 100% DECISION

"Once you learn to quit, it becomes a habit."
-Vince Lombardi

I started by going to the gym three days a week. I was dreading it. I would look for excuses not to "deal with it today." I told myself *I can skip and make up for it on the weekend*—I never did, of course. But then something started to shift. In an effort to lose weight, I committed to 4 days a week. That's when I realized the benefits I didn't see coming and started to enjoy it, look forward to it, and even prioritize it. It helped me with anxiety before a big presentation at work. It helped me with productivity throughout the day if I tackled it in the morning. I was in better moods and felt a sense of accomplishment that helped me want to continue the momentum.

The final shift was making a 100% decision: I go to the gym. Every day. Sure, from time to time I take a day off or find alternative ways to get in exercise BUT I am 100% committed to value and prioritize exercise daily. I've seen the progress in my health and my mentality has permanently shifted. This is how you tackle your personal finances. You start small. You face your fears. You educate yourself. You gain momentum. Chores become routine. Routine becomes the new norm. Success begets success.

I'm not asking you to make a 100% decision today, this week, or even this month. I want you to grow into it naturally. Otherwise, you might call it a "money diet" and, as we all know, most diets fail. We focus on the action and not the why. We focus on rules and not the goal. Hacks, like the 100% decisions, work because they are not rigid rules. They work because they are fun and repeatable. Try as many money hacks as you can, repeat what works, and you might just find yourself building routines and daily habits that stick.

Just like working out, my finances are my priority. Making good financial decisions is now a permanent part of my identity. Everything shifts when you commit 100%.

7. START WITH THE END IN MIND

As we end the first chapter, we're really just getting started. Heck, we've hardly talked about specific money hacks! Instead, I hope that I've grounded you in a mindset that will help you frame your financial journey with purpose, creativity, productivity, and commitment. This is the perfect time to reset and reflect before diving into the details: What are you hoping to learn by the time you finish this book? What is your why? If you spent just 5 minutes a day (including the weekend) committing to getting 1% better and you did "just one thing" every day (*seriously*, including the weekend!) what could YOU accomplish this week? This month? This year? Write it down, and commit to it 100%.

Wealth is relative to what you want. Knowing what you want can be difficult to pinpoint and even changes over time. So, in this moment, try asking yourself: "How much is enough?" This is how you start with the end in mind.

Studies have been done on this topic of "enough" in very specific terms. In 2010, Princeton University found that having money did increase happiness levels, but not beyond $75,000 annually. There was not any greater degree of happiness reported beyond that number. Great. Now you know your number, right? Well, not exactly…

The truth is, your income level is irrelevant if your spending is out of control or if you lack knowledge when it comes to making your savings grow and compound over time. Not to mention, your number might vary widely depending on whether you live in a high cost of living area, or if you support a family. There isn't necessarily one magic number to aim for. So, rather than focusing on a number, I want you to shift your mindset to know that you can be happy if you have two things: education and a willingness to take action. With those two foundational pieces, you can create a plan. I'm not naive. I understand there is no one-size-fits-all solution. That's where creativity comes into play.

Here's the plan: determine your why. Get educated and committed. Adjust your mindset and believe in yourself. That's what this book is all about. Because there is one thing I know: creativity beats inaction every day of the week. So let's take action and start hackin'.

Read next: "The One Thing" by Gary Keller and Jay Papasan

CHAPTER TWO

Debt & Credit Hacks

Only 1 in 4 millennials are debt-free according to a 2018 survey by life-insurance company Northwestern Mutual. 41% of those surveyed claimed their debt came from a combination of student loans and credit cards. According to The Motley Fool, 65% of Americans in debt have no idea when they'll shed it. It gets worse… 25% of those in debt expect to die before it's paid off. While that sounds dark, a healthy percentage of those are speaking to their mortgage, which is generally more acceptable and palatable in terms of debt. But still!

We're not done being bleak yet! According to the book "Financial Freedom" by Grant Sabatier, the average American household has $15,654 in credit card debt, $27,669 in auto loan debt, and $46,597 in student loan debt. Ouch.

Talking about debt can be overwhelming so before we begin, remember that your debt does not control you. You can take control back. And just like all things money, I truly believe there's a hack for that. In an effort to end on a positive note, there's one habit we can learn from the wealthy. Chris Hogan, author of "Everyday Millionaires", found that 73% of millionaires have never carried a credit card balance in their lives. Perhaps this tells us if we want to be millionaires, shedding all credit card debt (and keeping it off) is step one. Let's discuss how!

8. PAY OFF YOUR DEBTS IN THIS ORDER

I'm a realist. I understand there are many factors to consider when creating a debt payoff plan. Timing and strategies may differ depending on your interest rates, balance amounts, and goals. With that said, here is a straightforward plan if you're struggling to get your head around the order of operations for multiple debts. I recommend you prioritize paying off your debts in this order:

- High-interest consumer debt, like credit cards or (...*gulp*...) payday loans
- Debts that are keeping you up at night, like money owed to friends or family
- Personal or business loans
- Student loans
- Mortgage

Again, this is not a fool-proof plan but I highly recommend you get rid of credit card debts and debts that are keeping you up at night first. From there, personal loans, like for a car, or small business loans might take priority. Student loan debt is extremely important to prioritize sooner if you have a high balance or high interest (comparatively) and your other debts are low. Even though the interest rates for student loans are low compared to consumer debts, a high balance may mean you end up paying double what you borrowed. In some cases, it could be *triple*. And finally, a mortgage is often your lowest interest loan. If you're on a typical 30-year mortgage, try to pay a little extra on the principal when you can to take advantage of lower interest overall. More on this in Section 2. Of course, while paying off your debts it's important to also prioritize building an emergency fund of ideally 3 to 6 months of living expenses so that you don't have to automatically turn to high-interest credit card debt in the future.

In "The Money Resolution", I covered the *snowball* and *avalanche* methods for paying off debt. In a nutshell, with the snowball method, you line up your debts and pay off the one with the lowest *balance*, disregarding interest rates. With the avalanche method, you line up your debts and prioritize paying off the one with the highest *interest* rate first, ignoring the balance.

There's one more strategy I learned about recently that's worth consideration. The *debt tsunami* method forces you to rank your debts in order of personal importance. In other words, prioritize paying off the debts that are keeping you up at night the *most*. For example, owing money to a friend or family member might be weighing on your mind more than your high balance credit card debt that is accruing interest. Even if interest isn't accruing, you may feel better prioritizing your most emotional debt. Lifting this weight could be the momentum you need to help you tackle your other debts. After that, you might want to consider the debt snowball or debt avalanche method for remaining debts.

Here's the big takeaway: money is emotional. Humans are emotional. Tapping into your emotions is essential when it comes to money and debt. Personal finance is one part math, eight parts emotion, and one part action. The snowball and tsunami methods are good reminders that emotion, for example, the feeling of relief in fully paying off a debt, is a very important and valid factor in money-making decisions. While the avalanche method might make the most mathematical, fiscal sense, any of these methods are valid and you should choose the one that works best for you and will keep you on track.

9. TRY THESE CREDIT CARD PAYOFF STRATEGIES

We've already covered the debt snowball and avalanche methods. We've also introduced the debt tsunami method. A great, stormy appetizer. But for the main course, here are 5 specific strategies and tools to help you pay off your debts faster. These tips work rain or shine!

Make frequent and small credit card payments.
This hack can really help if you're struggling with managing your debt. Instead of waiting until your next paycheck to see what is leftover, prioritize your credit card payments by sending a little bit of

your cash on hand towards that balance every few days.

Use a debt payoff calculator to create a strategy.

With a quick internet search, I came across a super straightforward credit card debt payoff calculator from NerdWallet. You can add multiple cards and debts, enter the interest rates, and submit the minimum to see when you'll be able to pay these off and how much interest will accrue over that time. THEN the calculator asks you something very important: "How much extra money can you pay each month?" This is powerful. As you move the toggle, you can see how dramatically the total interest can shrink and how many years of payment you can shave off. Knowledge is power.

Transfer your balance to a no-interest promotional card.

The specifics on how to do this safely and for maximum benefit were covered in my book, "The Money Resolution" and in the video mentioned below. In short, a balance transfer allows you to transfer your high-interest balance to a new low or no-interest credit card. Typically you won't accrue interest in the first year or more, so you have that window to aggressively pay off your debt without paying a penny more.

Get a personal loan and consolidate.

Personal loans typically have interest rates in the low double digits. However, with good credit, you may have access to a personal loan in the 5-6% range. If so, or even if the rate is lower than your current loan, this could help you consolidate and get rid of your bad, high-interest debt immediately. Just make sure you establish a timeline and use smart strategies to pay off this personal loan! And, as always, do some research before making any serious financial decisions regarding your personal finances and debt.

Don't forget, no matter what strategy you use to pay off your debt, try your absolutely hardest to curb your spending and NOT add to your debt during the payoff process. One funny hack I heard about from a friend was literally freezing your credit card in a block of ice. That way, if you really want to use it, you'll need to wait thirty minutes or so for your card to thaw out. By then, you'll realize that you're probably overspending.

Watch next on YouTube: The Money Resolution "How To Tackle Your Credit Card Debt"

10. DIVERT YOUR SAVINGS

Every time you end a subscription or otherwise save (think: reducing insurance costs, cutting the cable cord, moving to a family cell phone plan), send these savings towards your debt. Immediately. It's one thing to save, it's another thing to tell your savings what to do. When you think about it, you're saving twice—once by reducing or eliminating a bill, and again by paying off debt that would be otherwise accruing interest. Say it with me: Reduce your expenses then divert the savings towards debt. And voila! Two birds, one hack!

A small twist on this would be to divert any additional income you earn towards your debts. This could come in the form of a raise or a new side hustle (see Chapter 9 for how to make money online). It's absolutely critical you have a plan for a windfall or increasing income. Otherwise, you're a prime candidate to fall victim to lifestyle creep— where you spend more as you earn more—and no one has room in their life for creeps.

11. BOOST YOUR CREDIT SCORE

A good credit score can unlock savings and benefits like insurance discounts, access to loans, and credit card rates with favorable returns. And if good is good, great is better! There's an easy button for that, right? Absolutely not.

Increasing your credit score takes blood, sweat, and tears, but most importantly *time*. Okay, maybe not blood… but, believe it or not, there are specific strategies to boost your credit score that are low effort and high impact. There are many ways to skin the... credit score. Here are 8 I found to be most useful:

Pay down credit card debt.

A low utilization ratio is what you should aim for. Meaning, the less you use your credit the better. You don't need to carry a balance. That is an ugly myth that you need to wipe out of your memory. A "no utilization" ratio is best-est! But keep in mind, an inactive account may get shut down which will negatively impact your score. If your oldest credit card is canceled, that's even worse because "average credit length" comprises 15% of your overall credit score mix. Curious about the other 85%? Learn more at myfico.com.

Schedule credit card payments wisely.

Pay off your card before your card's closing date if possible. Your closing date is what is reported to credit agencies, not your payment due date. This keeps your utilization down. Simply put, try to pay off as much of your balance as soon as possible (before the closing date) and earlier than is required, for reporting purposes.

Ask for a credit limit raise.

Using a low percentage of your available credit shows restraint. Restraint is good in the eyes of lenders. They want to see that you are responsible for leaving money on the table that others may be tempted to use. Typically, card issuers will increase your limit a small amount once a year, but you can try contacting your card companies directly to request a limit increase. This, in turn, can also lower your credit utilization ratio and improve your overall score.

Pay bills by the due date.

Do this without exception. Never, ever miss a minimum payment on a credit card. As an aside, it's always worth digging through your credit report to make sure there aren't any errors. If a payment appears missed that wasn't, your score could be affected and the issue could be easily fixable.

Apply for credit cautiously and infrequently.
This one is simple. Don't sign up for multiple credit cards or take out multiple loans close together, unless you really, *really* know what you are doing.

Find inaccurate information on your credit report and have it removed.
Start with checking your credit report. You can do this for free annually from each of the major credit agencies at www.annualcreditreport.com. According to a study conducted by the Federal Trade Commission, 1 in 5 people have an error on at least one of their credit reports. Find something off? It could be an error or identity theft. Contact your lender and rectify it. This could mean up to a 40-point pop on your credit score!

Leverage someone else's good credit.
If you have little to no credit, first off, good on you for reading a finance book! Second, this is a great tip for you: if you have a parent with good credit and they add you as an authorized user on a credit card account, their account history will show up on your report.

Just give it time...
Good habits and time are your friends. What's done is done. But good, consistent habits will pay off in due time. Be patient and keep an eye on that score as it slowly creeps up. Best of all, seeing it improve is a great, tangible way to achieve an early win. Once again, success begets success!

Tackling debt effectively is an essential first step in increasing your net worth, but the fun *really* begins when you start saving money wisely. Let's beget more success and cover savings hacks!

CHAPTER THREE

Savings Hacks

"Money in the bank is like toothpaste in the tube.
Easy to take out, hard to put back."
-Earl Wilson

In 2019, 23% of Americans report they put 0% of their monthly paycheck toward savings. And, likely because of this, a quarter of Americans have no retirement savings at all. 13% say credit card debt prevents them from saving. 13% say student loan debt prevents them from saving (more on student loans in Chapter 16). On top of that, 24% withdraw from their savings account once a month (Forbes). I really want to sprinkle in some good news but facts are facts...

The Washington Post reported:
- The average millennial has an average net worth of $8,000. Far less than previous generations.
- A 2019 study showed two out of three millennials don't have anything saved for retirement.
- 69% of Americans have less than $1,000 in savings. 34% have no savings at all.
- 18% of Americans spend more than they save. (If I'm being honest, I suspect it's far worse than that...)

Why prioritize saving your money? If you don't prioritize your money, someone else will. Personally, I learned to find as much joy, if not more, in saving than I ever did in spending.

So, stop comparing your situation with the facts above and start getting creative when it comes to saving. And fear not because: savings, there's a hack for that too.

12. CREATE GOALS, AUTOMATE YOUR WAY TO THEM

If the three most important words in real estate are *location, location, location*, the three most important words in savings are *automate, automate, automate*. Here is how to do so without fail.

According to the same Forbes study referenced above, 63% of Americans do not set annual savings goals. Even those that do may not necessarily create the right system to achieve their goals. Creating a goal, assigning a completion date, and leveraging automation are actually quite simple. It's even easier if you break it down into parts. If you decide to save $10,000 in one year for your emergency fund, you divide that number by 12 months and find out that you need to set aside $833.33 every month in order to achieve this goal. If you want to leverage automation and you get paid twice a month, you need to divert $416.67 each payday to an emergency fund *automatically*. That's roughly $192 a week. That $10,000 goal doesn't sound so far-fetched now, does it? But the truth is, even if this *sounds* doable, none of us are likely to remember to do this manually each and every paycheck. That's why we must set up automation.

One way to do this is within your own main bank account with just a few clicks online by setting up a second savings account. From there, you can either split where your funds are paid via direct deposit or you can set up automation within your bank account if that feature is available. The former might require a form or two through your employer. Even *better* is using this strategy paired with an online-only high-yield savings account. There are hundreds of options and rates are always changing but some quick research can help you find the current best rates and ones that others recommend.

The idea behind automation is to prevent you from making the choice between spending or saving your money. By putting your financial plan on autopilot, you are able to direct your funds as soon as they hit your account. The best way to save towards retirement, a debt-repayment plan, or your emergency fund is to do it automatically so you don't have to do anything at all. Set it and forget it! It will not only help you build wealth, but it'll save you time and mental energy.

Once again, set your goal and create your system for achieving your goal. It might feel uncomfortable for a few paychecks but future you won't just thank you—future you will give you a big hug. That's a metaphor. Picturing it is weird I'll admit...

Pro Tip: Use the emergency fund calculator from NerdWallet to help you find the amount of money you need saved to cover six months of expenses when life inevitably punches you in the face. You know what to do after that!

Read On: CNBC "38-year-old retired millionaire: One simple habit leads to wealth"

13. REWARD YOURSELF, SAVE IT INSTEAD

In an interview with CNBC Make It, figure skater Adam Rippon explained his number one trick for saving money. He said, "I'll see something that I really like and kind of want, and then I take a step back and I'm like, you know what, I don't really need it. So, then I do this... I see how much the price was of the thing I wanted and I take it out of my account and I put it right into my savings. If I felt like I could live without that chunk of money, then I'm going to take it out of the account like I bought it but I'm going to put it in my savings account. It works... because you still have that exhilarating 'this is a lot of money' feeling but you're just moving money around."

For Adam, these little *almost-splurged-but-I-saved-instead* moments might lead to hundreds or even thousands of dollars socked away. But, even if you're not a wealthy professional athlete, you could apply this same principle to avoiding everyday non-necessary purchases. Escape Target or Ikea with JUST the items on your list? Reward your savings by diverting the funds you nearly spent to your savings account!

Similarly, if you are making a big purchase do extensive research. Be patient. If that product goes on sale and you have saved up the funds for it, bank the money you saved. You can also apply this concept to bigger wins like canceling a subscription, disconnecting a service, or paying off debt. Divert that now-defunct monthly payment into savings. Cut the cord and replaced it with a cheaper streaming option? Pocket the difference. Done paying $50 a month to get out of credit card debt? Keep paying $50... to yourself! Don't stop there... If you earn a 5% raise, boost your 401(k) or IRA contribution by that same amount. Even if you tuck away just 3%, you'll still see a little extra in your paycheck while putting most of your raise to work for future you.

Resisting a splurge purchase, finding a great deal, or earning a raise is a great start. Pocketing that money into savings makes for an easy, pain-free hack.

Watch Next on YouTube: CNBC Make It "Figure Skater Adam Rippon's No. 1 Trick For Saving Money"

14. BANK 100% OF YOUR WINDFALLS

According to Forbes, 39% of Americans in 2019 planned on putting their tax refund directly in savings. That is a surprisingly positive statistic! And yet, sadly, I don't believe it...

Be honest. What do you usually do with your tax refund? I know most of my friends would answer with something similar to, "Splurge on something I really want and put the rest towards my student loans." Admirable and on the right track. You earned it after all, right? Wrong. You loaned the government your money at no interest throughout the year and you're finally getting paid back. That's your money and if you had invested it, it could have grown! Don't be tempted to spend any.

However, if you don't trust yourself with that tax refund, one thing you might want to consider doing is deferring your refund until next year. In other words, if you are owed $500, you can wait to receive your $500 back until next year. This is one way to pay your future self, especially if you think there's a possibility you might owe taxes in the upcoming year.

Earn a bonus at work? Awesome! Send 100% of it towards your savings or boost your emergency fund (more on this in a moment). At the very least, tuck it away. Period. Pretend it never happened. This will feel tough the first time you do it. However, after you do this a few times, you just built a habit. And habits are the very best friends anyone could have.

15. TAKE A MONEY-SAVING CHALLENGE

There are a ton of daily and weekly savings challenges all over the internet, just give it a search. As an example, there is one in which you save $1 in week 1. In week 2, you set aside $2. And so on. While you could do this IRL using coins, cash, and a piggy bank, that's probably not very realistic. Instead, I recommend you set this daily change aside through an FDIC-insured app like Tip Yourself. Even better, you won't be tempted to break into your jar when you're craving something you don't need like a fancy meal out or that new blanket hoodie with bear ears from that infomercial...

Here's another example: Start by saving a nickel. Save that amount but add 5 additional cents every day. If you are consistent and DON'T miss a day, this "change" adds up to $3,339.75 in a year. And, the most you'll ever have to save in a day is $18.25. Keep in mind, savings are back-loaded with this challenge so you'll be saving the most towards the end of the challenge.

I personally like the challenges that have a bit of randomness to them, rather than starting tiny and ending more extreme. This way, you aren't starting super easy and tempted to give up when it gets to be too much. Either way, have a goal in mind when you begin and find a savings challenge to help you get there. Once you complete a challenge, try another! Eventually, you're likely to develop systems that stick when it comes to setting aside a little bit of money every day or every week. Bonus points if you find a way to automate this and pay yourself first!

> **Pro Tip:** Take a challenge with a friend! It's definitely more fun to save when you aren't going at it alone. Plus, you can encourage each other and hold each other accountable!

16. DOUBLE YOUR EMERGENCY FUND

Here's some seemingly good news: according to Forbes, 40% of Americans prioritize their savings for their emergency fund. On the surface that sounds great. 40% put their emergency fund first?! No, not exactly. Re-read that... 40% prioritize their *savings for* their emergency fund. In other words, of those that are actually saving, 40% prioritize an emergency fund. In addition, 49% report they only have enough liquid funds (cash on hand) to cover living expenses for zero to three months. I'm going to guess that a good portion of that 49% is closer to the zero month side, not three.

Here's the problem, even those that prioritize aren't saving enough. Whatever you think you need, some say 3-6 months of living expenses, you need to double it. Trust me. I learned this lesson the hard way earlier this year. I hesitate to share this story because it's sad and involves a dog (skip the next paragraph if you wish!) but it's a great example to prove the point.

I'll spare the details, but my 9-year young border collie Tucker developed a brain tumor and I didn't have pet insurance. By the time we discovered the tumor, I had already spent $4,000 on exams and scans, the bulk of my $5,000 emergency fund. After I indicated I was willing to do whatever it took, the specialist estimated surgery would cost $8,000 to $10,000. Radiation would only cost $4,000-$6,000 *if* I traveled across the state and relocated to Washington State University for a month. Otherwise, double that. Add another $1,000 or more for relocating. I chose the radiation route but he sadly passed away the afternoon before he was set to begin. $6,500 later, I had more than depleted my emergency fund while saying farewell to my sweet angel of a pup. Of course, I would have rather gone into debt and still had him here but, regardless of the outcome, the story illustrates an unexpected emergency, one that goes beyond typical living expenses. In my mind, an emergency was "losing a job". I gravely underestimated what life can, and inevitably will, throw at you.

As a palate cleanser, here are a few great things in life: waking up to good weather on the weekend, finding $5 on the sidewalk, a cold beer or glass of wine after a long day of work, and your team winning the Super Bowl.

For my new emergency fund, I use a combination of Betterment and Acorns because they leverage two powerful savings concepts: automation and growth via safe investing. No matter where you choose to save your money, I recommend you keep it out of sight and out of mind to remove any temptation to touch it.

What's the minimum you should have tucked away for an emergency? According to a recent report from CNBC, two economists suggest the minimum emergency fund for low-income households should be $2,467—only about one month of a $30,000 annual salary. If you make more than $30,000, this is not nearly enough. I'd argue you need at least 3-6 months. And again, double whatever number you arrive at. You will not regret it.

> **Pro Tip:** Once you've doubled what you think you might need in an extreme emergency, start a personal equity fund. This is money you can allow yourself to spend on yourself for personal development. This includes online courses, conferences, books you can't find at your local library, in-person classes at a local college, and even something like a gym membership if you're setting a fitness goal. A personal equity fund allows you to have guilt-free spending on things that will improve your quality of life, because of course life is for living.

17. STARVE AND STACK

This is a hack for couples tackling money goals together. The essential idea here is to live off of one income and use the other to tackle finances. According to Nick Vail of Remove the Guesswork, who coined the term "starve and stack", this is a perfect strategy for newlyweds during their first 18-24 months of marriage and combined finances. It doesn't have to be forever. But 18-24 months of almost extreme frugal living could help your family unit pay off student loan debt, create a nest egg investment, or save up a down payment on a house.

First of all, and I cannot stress this point enough: it's essential to communicate about money with your significant other and align on goals, priorities, and a plan. It's widely known that money is the number one reason why married couples divorce.

With that said, if you both have a steady income, this is an interesting exercise to go through. Sit down and see what it would take to live off of just ONE of those incomes. Start with the larger of the two. If it doesn't look too scary, see what it would look like to live off of the lower of the two. This is the best-case scenario and the ultimate saving hack.

While it might sound extreme if this is a new concept to you, on paper, it might not look as impossible—especially if you're able to combine it with other strategies in this chapter and book. The next step is committing to one of the two options and actually giving it a shot! But there's one more critical step... what are you going to do with the other income? This, again, goes back to mutual goals. Do you want to eliminate all debt? Are you saving for a down payment for a house? Are you looking to boost your retirement? Are you considering kids in your future? Ideally, this is the first conversation you have. The how-to comes next and the "starve and stack" method might be your how-to! And don't worry, there is no actual starving happening here. Just smart planning, budgeting, and living below your means!

It can also work well for individuals with a side hustle. The ultimate goal would be to live off of your side hustle and save all of your professional job income.

18. DON'T LOSE SIGHT OF YOUR NUMBERS

This isn't a figure of speech. I mean *literally* don't lose sight of your numbers (or your goals!). Here are some fun ways you can do this:

- Create a custom credit card with a representation of your goal printed directly on it! The next time you go to swipe your card you might think twice about that purchase when you glance at it.
- Change your desktop or phone screen to something related to your goals like a picture of your upcoming beach vacation or the car you're saving up for.
- Create passwords that remind you of your goals. Example: d3btFre3JaN1. And now I have to go change all my passwords...
- Keep a sign on your desk about your Why or create a basic post-it note and attach it to your monitor. Heck, print your goal and frame it in your office like a beautiful piece of art.
- Label your alarm clock with your goal so it's the first thing you see in the morning. Bonus: it might prevent you from hitting snooze!

Visualization is key, so get creative and keep your numbers and goals visible. Even better if it's public. Although I'll admit, I got some strange looks when I turned my Zoom background into a Dyson vacuum...

Pro Tip: Try a Debt Free Chart, created by Heidi Ifland Nash. Heidi was in the process of paying off $38,000 in debt when she created a coloring chart to help her track her progress. She'd color in another section every time she made a payment until the page was filled and her debt was paid off. For her, visualizing the process was powerful and went a long way in helping her stay motivated. She decided to help others with their own financial milestones by taking requests and creating customized savings and payoff charts. She now offers more than 100 debt-free chart designs from saving up for an emergency fund to paying off your car loans. Find them at debtfreecharts.com. Prices range from FREE to $2.00. More on my favorite four-letter f-word in Chapter 11. (..."Free" to be clear. Get your head out of the gutter!)

***

CHAPTER FOUR

Frugality Hacks

"Price is what you pay, value is what you get"
-Warren Buffett

Some scoff at the idea of pinching pennies but penny-pinching does turn into dollars. And dollar-pinching turns into hundreds of dollars. Plus, it builds positive and lasting habits.

In my year of getting my financial life together, I was shocked to see the massive savings when I committed to making my own coffee and bringing my lunch to work every day. That momentum led to several phone calls to bring down my insurance payments, credit card interest rates, and other bills. I documented it all and shared my best tips in my first book, "The Money Resolution".

In "The Money Resolution", I preached small steps. I believe that small efforts day in and day out help build good habits and in turn, build savings. And it really does work! I even had a reader tell me they tallied up their savings from taking the advice and actions from my book and that number was $4,000. Awesome.

I know it's not realistic to just not buy stuff. We're human. And sometimes we do just crave *things*. But here are some creative hacks that will help you buy fewer things and save on others. At the very least, cutting back will provide a little breathing room if you are living paycheck to paycheck. So let's get to dollar-pinching.

19. CREATE A MONEY ROADBLOCK

Just the other day we were driving to my hometown of Tacoma, Washington to go to my niece's musical when, of course, we got stuck because a drawbridge was up—5 minutes into our 60-minute drive… I quickly declared, "Nope, I'm never driving again." While admittedly dramatic (especially because I was in the passenger seat), the core issue I was struggling with was my frustration about the amount of effort it was taking to get from point A to point B. Several years ago, I couldn't deal with the struggle anymore. I made the decision to ditch my car and buy a Vespa. I had had enough of sitting in traffic and dealing with parking and yes, even hitting literal roadblocks due to construction. And by the way, there's construction EVERYWHERE in Seattle. Okay, this was therapeutic to write down but let's tie this back to frugality…

Money roadblocks work similarly. They slow you down from point A (oh, that looks pretty I NEED now!) to point B (checkout with 1-click). So how do you create a roadblock? Let me count the ways!

- Remove your credit card information from your phone's wallet and any online-shopping websites.
- Remove your bank account info from Paypal, Venmo, Google Pay, Cash, Take My Money Out Of Sight Out Of Mind apps. While not real, I might be onto something with that last one!
- Leave your wallet at home when you're "just going for a walk" in your favorite neighborhood that includes your favorite record store and bookstore… okay yes, this one is personal.
- "Pay yourself first" directly into your retirement and savings accounts so, you know, you literally DON'T have the money readily available.
- Take out cash and use only that amount. This is especially useful at events where you might be tempted to get "just one more drink." However, I will admit, this may become more and more difficult as, at least in Seattle, I'm starting to see more and more "we don't accept cash" signs.

There are so many more ways but you get the idea. Technology has made it increasingly easy to spend money at the tip of a finger tap or slide, requiring little to no thought on our end. Force yourself to take one or two extra steps. Or you might just find yourself shopping online next time you're stuck when the bridge is up.

20. ASK YOURSELF: CAN I AFFORD 5?

"Whatever it is, we're probably not buying it"
-Mrs. Frugalwoods

This one is super simple. Any time you're tempted to buy something you ~~need~~ want, ask yourself if you could afford to buy 5 today. Why? This helps you quickly understand the impact of splurge purchases. If you can't afford five of this exact item, you shouldn't buy one. Five splurge purchases add up incredibly fast. Sure, this one thing doesn't seem like a big deal in the grand scheme of things. But if you made this one (bad) decision 5 times today, this week, or even this month, you are very likely to regret it. This is especially useful when it comes to clothes, shoes, technology (looking at you, new Beats headphones...), tickets to a ballgame or show, eating out, and 50 times over when walking through IKEA.

Instead, focus on practicing mindful spending. Consider why you really wanted the thing or things in the first place and how it fits in with your goals. You don't need to budget every dollar. But you should always work on cutting back on impulse purchases and asking yourself this one question could offer just the pause you need so that logic can trump impulse.

Pro Tip: Use the shortcuts in IKEA to get to where you need to go for the thing (not things) you need. Or start at the exit if you know the location of the piece of furniture you're there to get. Or wear a blindfold and have someone guide you. Or just, you know, don't go in there at all—especially on payday!

---

21. CALCULATE COST IN HOURS

We often think about our income and paycheck as one lump sum earned. However, the reality is that paycheck is earned by the day and by the hour. When you understand your hourly rate and compare that to your purchases and potential purchases, it might be the reality check you need when you're tempted to buy something you don't actually need. If you make $25 an hour, those $100 shoes cost you 4 hours. That $1,500 laptop equals 60 hours of your time. That $25,000 car would cost you 1,000 hours. All of this, of course, is excluding tax, shipping, and interest if you aren't paying in cash. Would you trade 1,000 working hours—equivalent to *25 weeks at work*—for that new car?

On the one hand, you might be thinking, *just 60 hours and I can get a brand new laptop*? Well, yes. However, when you look at your paycheck and break out how many hours are needed towards your expenses and savings, you are likely to realize you only have a few hours of your pay period that are truly disposable for "want" purchases. If that's the case, those shoes are the ONLY splurge purchase you can make this paycheck. That laptop means saving for 20 paychecks. That car? Just 333 months and you can own it outright in cash! Doesn't feel so doable now, does it?

Of course, there is hope. We'll cover Earning and Spending in future chapters!

> **Pro Tip**: Install the Chrome extension "Time Well $pent." This helps you (not) shop by understanding how much time something costs. It literally replaces prices with time, based on your hourly wage. It's a great way to think of your money in terms of hours spent to earn the money you're considering spending!

22. FACTOR IN DEPRECIATION

This does not require real math. There's no secret formula to apply to all of your purchases to determine their future value—nor would anyone have the time for that. The key is to understand that liabilities depreciate over time (a liability is anything that loses value over time). A car is the simplest example. A car is not an asset (an asset is anything that gains value over time). You've heard this before but it's true: a brand new car loses 10% of its value within a month of the moment you drove it off the lot. It will continue to lose 15%-20% of its value each year after.

It's extremely important that you consider depreciation while making big purchases. What's a big purchase? That's up to you to define but personally, any single item over $50 is considered a big purchase to me. The key is to ask yourself, "Will I be able to resell this when I'm done using it?" and if yes, "How much could I resell this item for?" If the answers are "No" or "Yes, for very little", this is the perfect time to ask yourself, "Do I really need this item?", "Could I borrow this item?", and "Could I live without this item?" Chances are it's not a need and you can, and should, do without it.

I'm not asking you to pause and think about depreciation with every single item you buy. But this quick check can go a long way. Here are other big purchase examples that deserve a pause and question regarding depreciation: new clothes and shoes, season tickets supporting a sports team on the decline, digital media like video games you can't resell, brand new furniture, or tickets to Hamilton. Obviously kidding about the last one. I for one am not going to waste my one shot... to buy those.

23. WORK FROM HOME

This has been the ultimate hack for me. In mid-2018, I was offered a position at a company where most employees work remotely. I did not know this was the case throughout the interview process. Little did I know, that phone call with the offer from HR which included the question, "How comfortable are you working remotely?" was going to be life-changing.

When people ask me about working from home they usually key

in on questions related to sleep, productivity, and office culture. Yes, I probably get a little more sleep. I'm actually *more* productive without coworker interruptions and more in-person meetings and check-ins filling up my time. And yes, sometimes I miss office culture but that's always there if I need it and choose to go into the office. What others don't tend to key in on is the savings (and general satisfaction!) that come with working from home.

I wake up to a luxurious homemade iced or pour-over coffee and have my choice of whatever sounds good for breakfast, no more sad protein bar wolfed down as I scramble to catch the bus, miss the bus, and then pay $20 (minimum) for parking in downtown Seattle. For lunch, I eat leftovers from dinner or make a delicious sandwich, sometimes with fresh bacon. Yum. If the weather is nice, I'll enjoy lunch outside with my pup or we'll even go for a stroll (saving money on a dog walker). I spend zero on transportation. I have no commute. I get hours of time back every week by not traveling, not to mention the cost of bus fare, parking, and gas. I walk a few blocks to the gym in the afternoon to clear my head and refocus. I fold laundry while waiting for something I have to have before completing a critical task (while watching my email and listening in on meetings). I don't have to worry about accruing enough hours to take a vacation because, worst case, I can work from anywhere. I'm able to stop my work at the end of the day and immediately transition to working on a YouTube video or writing for my own projects. You get the idea...

Working from home was a game-changer for me and it could be for you. Read "The 4-Hour Workweek" by Tim Ferris if you don't believe me. Then, figure out if you can negotiate a day at home each week or look for a fully-remote job. I will say it's not for everyone, especially those that crave human interaction IRL or are in a career that requires being on-site. But, if you have an opportunity to work from home, give it a shot! Your wallet and your wellbeing will thank you.

24. REPAIR OR FIX, DON'T REPLACE

I am by no means a handyman. I know how to use a screwdriver and a hammer, on a good day. I once mounted two TVs in ONE DAY and that was a major accomplishment. In other words, it might be odd to hear this advice from someone with very little skill when it comes to channeling his inner Tim "The Toolman" Taylor. But when it comes to worn, dirty, or broken things around the home, you should consider asking yourself, "Can I fix this?" If the answer is maybe, ask for help or look online for ideas.

A few months back my girlfriend finally decided it was time to replace our living room rug. Once upon a time, it was white. Two years later it was... well, honestly I don't know what color(s) you would call that. It was shades of tan, grey, mauve, and taupe. The problem was, we had guests coming over that night and had a full list of "to-dos" ahead of us. Instead of shopping and splurging at the last minute, we decided to break out the Resolve and a hefty dose of elbow grease. I cannot report that it looked perfect or that we *never* replaced it but we invited it to our party that night.

How else could you get creative when your thing in question is on the fritz? Here are a few more examples:

- Replace the dead battery in your laptop or watch before using this as an excuse to buy new.
- Watch a YouTube video and see if you can't fix that leaky faucet before calling a plumber.
- Get a cheap plastic version of a "snake" tool and unclog your shower drain.
- Learn how to change a tire or jump a car's dead battery.
- Clean, clean, clean when your lease is up so you don't get charged a cleaning fee. This might require paint touch-up or replacing a broken outlet cover.

Now I have just one thing to ask you: "*Does everybody know what time it is?!*"

25. BE WILLING TO TRADE

I was so mad at myself for going PC over Mac when I started my new job. The company provides a "technology" stipend but that's because it's a B.Y.O.C. environment. I had always used a PC for work so I figured this was the best bet. Three months later, I couldn't stand my Dell XPS and was ready to do something about it.

The problem? Even used MacBook Pros (my non-negotiables were 15", 2015 or newer) were running $1,500 on up to $2,500. I'd have to buy that AND deal with selling my Dell. After two weeks of looking and laughing at insane prices, I had an epiphany. I just had to Think Different—sorry I couldn't help it. I decided to put up a post "WTT (willing to trade) my Dell XPS 15 for MacBook Pro 15" 2015 or newer." A week later and $200 out of pocket I was setting up my "new" MacBook. This computer has been a game-changer for me for my 9 to 5 and my 5 to 9.

If you're a frequent buyer and seller on Craigslist and are hitting a wall, think outside the box with your posts. Alternatively, I could have searched "WTT MacBook" and might have found someone else running into the same problem I had on the opposite end. Set yourself up a "WTT XYZ" alert and consider posting yourself. Look around your house and this might apply to entertainment as well. Have books, video games, board games, or clothes laying around you'd love to swap? Give it a shot! It might save you time, money, and stress!

26. LEARN TO ASK, SELL & BARTER

Salespeople don't close if they don't ask, just like you won't save if you don't ask for a discount. When is it appropriate? Always! Seriously. What's the worst that can happen? Someone will tell you no. Best case? The employee is in a great mood and scans a coupon they have handy or gives you a tip about where to find the item for cheap. Is this crazy? No! You'd be surprised how often you can save just by asking for a discount. I also suggest asking if a company will consider a competitor price match and never hesitate to request a return or refund even when you're beyond the return window. It's free to ask.

It's also incredibly powerful to learn to sell yourself. This can help you get out of a ticket, ace that interview, negotiate a raise, and so on. It's a skill to convince others that your point of view is a win-win. It starts with confidence. Believe in yourself and others will believe in you.

Finally, learn the art of barter. You have something someone else appreciates and wants. Others have something you appreciate and want. It's easy. Offer a swap! This can be skills, books, work benefits like discounts, or even herbs from your garden. Trade things, ideas, tips, food, you name it! Get creative and save yourself some money!

Pro Tip: Join a "Buy Nothing" group on Facebook. A buy nothing group is a great way to connect with locals in your area that have similar goals of spending less by giving and sharing. According to www.BuyNothingProject.org, "Buy Nothing Project rules are simple: Post anything you'd like to give away, lend, or share amongst neighbors. Ask for anything you'd like to receive for free or borrow. Keep it legal. No hate speech. No buying or selling, no trades or bartering, we're strictly a gift economy." I'll be honest, these are my kind of people!

***

PART 2

Hack The Big Three & Smaller Five

CHAPTER FIVE

Housing Hacks

Unfortunately, you can't frugal your way to riches. The reality is, if you want to get ahead you'll need to either A) earn more or B) curtail your spending by a substantial amount. Don't get me wrong, small efforts can add up over time and good habits are essential for building wealth, but if you want to really move the needle and fast, you'll need to tackle "The Big Three" head-on: Housing, Food, and Transportation. Many studies have revealed we spend roughly two-thirds of our take-home pay on The Big Three.

Let's start by tackling the biggest of the three: housing—from how to find an affordable place with less competition to mistakes to avoid when buying a house.

But first, some facts. According to a research study by home equity site Hometap:

- 73% of respondents admit to feeling "house rich, cash poor" at least some of the time.
- 60% of millennial homeowners say housing costs make it difficult to achieve their financial goals.
- Nearly 20% of millennial homeowners cite that 50-100% (100%??) of their monthly income goes to pay their mortgage.

Furthermore, a new study by TD Ameritrate in 2019 reports 50% of millennials were moving back with their parents post-college due to bleak financial situations, more Americans today than Gen X-ers.

The situation seems bleak. But it doesn't have to be. Because housing: there's a hack for that too!

27. RENT

Controversial right? While many people consider buying a house as an investment (and most of our parents cannot fathom why you wouldn't buy if you are in a position to do so) there can be many reasons to continue to rent instead, especially if you live in a high cost of living area. Here are five reasons renting can be more beneficial than buying:

Flexibility

Based on how interest is structured with a mortgage, it usually doesn't make financial sense to own for less than five years. Personally, that sounds like a long time to stay in one spot. I work from home. I could technically work anywhere in the world. So why would I want to put down long-term roots?

Maintenance

I'm no handyman and costs for sudden issues (not to mention routine maintenance) can be downright expensive. A recent coworker of mine told me about flooding in his basement. Next thing he knew, a private contractor was resetting the foundation in his house, a project that took many months and many, many dollars. No thank you…

Amenities

While I certainly don't live in a "luxury" apartment and my place has very little in the way of amenities—many big city apartment complexes come with a handful of the following: a gym, an office or coworking space, a rooftop with communal areas and a view, community rooms with pool tables and cable TV for gatherings that you can reserve for free, dog runs, fire pits, community events, and LOTS more. I like more… more is good!

Financial predictability

Sure, utilities will vary. Rent might go up at the end of your contract. And... nope. That's it. There's really nothing else to worry about in terms of sudden, unexpected costs. If your fridge suddenly goes out one day, your landlord is fully responsible for that repair and/or purchase. Plus, amenities mentioned above might save you the money you would have spent with a gym membership or at the coffee shop to find space to work.

Location, location, location

You like where you live and like what you have. I LOVE my neighborhood and there is no way I could afford to buy a home here. A modest starter home sells for over a million (I wish I were joking). I love my 100 square foot deck with a lake view. I have enough things to fill my 700 square foot apartment exactly and nothing more. I have relationships with my neighbors and property managers I'd hate to lose. The fact is, I fell in love with my apartment when I found it and I'm in no hurry to move on.

> **Pro Tip**: You can technically still invest in real estate in the form of REITs (Real Estate Investment Trusts), sometimes called "real estate stock". A REIT is a company that owns, operates, or finances income-producing properties, which generate a steady income stream for investors. Think offices, retail centers, hotels, apartment buildings, cell towers, data centers, warehouses, and the like. They are publicly traded like stocks and liquid, unlike owning physical real estate. An example of a fund I recommend is the VGSIX mutual fund. More on investing in Chapter 14.

Watch next on YouTube: Minority Mindset "Your house is not an investment"

28. TIPS FOR FINDING AFFORDABLE RENTALS

I won't bore you with the details but Seattle is expensive. For those in the know, you simply can't argue with me on that... therefore, I've gotten very creative over the years when it comes to hunting for a great unit at a great price.

Search photo-less listings for rentals

Sometimes you need to be a little more creative to get what you want or to find a diamond in the rough. That's where this hack comes in. Once you've landed on your non-negotiables and entered your filters in your Craigslist search, try unchecking the "photos" box that is selected by default. While there might be a good reason the property manager or homeowner decided not to post photos, oftentimes it's because the post is brand new or the poster isn't technologically savvy. Zig when others zag. You might want to request photos via email so you don't drive across town wasting your time, but this hack can definitely help you to snag a great place that everyone else is overlooking.

Consider the time of year

Look for rentals during slow times of the year, typically November through February. You'll have less competition which means you're more likely to land the lease and potentially get a better rate. If your current lease ends during a busy time of the year like the spring or summer, ask if you can move to a month-to-month agreement or consider a 6-month lease so that you can move your next lease to the off season.

Use Zillow

There aren't many websites or apps out there that are great for searching for rentals. Let's be honest, Craigslist is bloated with junk, false advertising, and creeps. Level up your hunt with Zillow. Redfin is my go-to when it comes to browsing houses for sale but Zillow is the cream of the crop in 2020 when it comes to finding quality rentals. It's a trusted site for great photos, great search filters, and accurate descriptions. I'm personally happy to recommend a local Seattle business, plus, I actually interviewed there once and I can personally attest to the fact that the people behind it are good people that care deeply about finding people good homes. I also appreciate the fact that they will message you updates based on your search preferences so you're the first to know when a new listing shows up that meets your criteria. It's almost as if I interviewed for an email marketing job...

But of course, the ultimate renting hack is to get a roommate. Or a partner. Look together and cut your housing costs in half!

29. LIVE WITH FAMILY

What an eye-roller, right? However, this hack could help you tackle all of The Big Three in one fell swoop. I don't care if you're 18 or 58, moving in with mom can be a fantastic setup. We need to get over the stereotype that living with your parents is embarrassing or you won't have a social life or you're admitting failure. You know deep down it checks lots of boxes and maybe you've thought about it once or twice. You even know deep down-er that your friends would be jealous, even if they'd never admit it. (Upon further reflection, if you're 58 you might consider having mom move in with you... but you get the point!)

A little tip or two or three if you do take the leap and move in with the 'rents:

Own it! Don't lie to others or yourself. Don't pretend it's "super temporary." You're making a small sacrifice that will pay off massively later! There's no shame in the living with the parents game, especially when you see how much you can save! In fact, quote me on this, *moving in with family is the 9th wonder of the world behind compound interest.* If only your mom made desserts like my mom...

Second, and I know you're moments from rolling your eyes, look at it as an opportunity to spend quality time together. Instead of focusing on the stigma, focus on the relationships and get to know one another better. None of us know how much time we have left together so be together!

And finally, don't expect a free ride. Pitch in and earn your keep. As my step dad always says, "nothing in life is free." Take on extra chores. Don't come home drunk. Cook for them every once in a while.

Buy a nice bouquet of flowers for them. And if they ever get on your nerves try out this hack: treat your mom like you do your best friend's mom. It works!

30. FIRST-TIME BUYER PROGRAMS

Let's say you're in a position where you're able to buy a home. Maybe you've lived with your parents for the last few years and you have a down payment ready and burning a hole in your pocket! First of all, please crunch your numbers and make sure homeownership is truly something you can take on. As I referenced before, nearly 1 out of 5 millennial homeowners spend 50-100% of their income on their mortgage. Don't forget the expenses of routine maintenance and necessary repairs. Can you *really* afford it? Use my favorite home buying calculator from NerdWallet to see how much home you can actually afford.

Assuming you've confirmed that you are indeed ready to take the leap, you should definitely look into first-time homebuyer programs offered by your county, state, or federally. Qualifying as a first-time homebuyer doesn't necessarily mean you've never owned a house. Meeting the qualifications unlocks many benefits, including low- or no-down-payment loans, down payment assistance, closing cost assistance, federal grants and more. Some home buyer assistance programs increase buyers' buying chances by prioritizing certain professions, such as educators, first responders, or veterans. Some programs give perks for homebuyers in certain geographic areas. And those perks can be worth a lot of money. The government REALLY wants you to be a homeowner, so if you're going that route you might as well take advantage of their programs.

> **Pro Tip**: In most cases, it doesn't make financial sense to buy a home if you plan to live there for less than 5 years. The majority of your mortgage payment each month at the start of your loan goes heavily towards interest, not the principal.

31. HOME BUYING HOUSE HUNTING HACKS

Buying a home is a big deal and can be an intimidating and daunting process. But, if being a homeowner or buying your next house is on your list of current life goals, here are a few hacks that many don't realize or think about:

- Gone are the days of needing 20% of the list price in cash as a down payment to purchase a home. You can put down as little as 3.5% and take out an FHA loan to make up the difference. The catch? You'll have to pay mandatory mortgage insurance, so it can cost more than a conventional loan. Just don't forget, you'll also need to cover closing costs (unless you're able to negotiate that the sellers pay), which can range from 2% to 5% of the home price.

- When touring a home, act uninterested. Realtors can smell your eagerness and will take advantage of the fact that you fell in love with the home by denying attempts at negotiation.

- Check your cell phone service while house hunting. It would be a huge bummer if you moved into a house where you couldn't get calls. This works while renting as well. I made this mistake once and had to switch providers, paying more out of pocket, due to a lack of service in my building.

- Don't borrow as much as the bank says you can afford. They don't have your best interests in mind... they just want all your money.

- As a rule of thumb, you should keep your monthly mortgage payment below 28% of your pre-tax income. Remember, the more you're able to put down upfront, the smaller your loan and the less your monthly payment will be.

- Stalk the neighborhood. Drive by during several times of the day and see what is happening in the community you're thinking about buying in. Want to know how friendly the neighbors are? A fun tip is simply to wave and smile at passersby and see if people wave back as you walk about.

- Don't make any major purchases or take any chances with your credit profile in the 3 to 6 months leading up to your home purchase. This includes opening new credit cards or amassing debt. Lenders want to see you as reliable.

These tips are just scratching the surface when it comes to buying a home and hacking the process. Continue on with your research and remember: buying a home isn't dating, it's a marriage. Take a long term view to maximize your investment and happiness.

32. HACK YOUR MORTGAGE PAYMENTS

So you have a house, and you have a mortgage. What's next? You could just dutifully pay your statement each month and not give it another thought. Or, you could hack it. I wonder which option I would suggest...

Make an extra mortgage payment each year
While it may be obvious to suggest that paying more than the minimum due to any debt will help you pay off a loan faster, this specific strategy in homeownership can easily be overlooked but has worked wonders for many. By strictly sticking to this strategy, you could slice years off your 30-year mortgage and save thousands upon thousands in interest. Want to go even more extreme? Pay $250, $500, even $1,000 extra each month. Depending on the balance of your loan, this could have a huge impact and help you own your home outright even sooner!

Pay the first 3 numbers
Assume you had a mortgage of $200,000. Use the first three numbers (in this case 200) to set the amount of your extra monthly payment. In this example, $200 extra every month will help you pay off a 30-year mortgage *8.5 years faster*. Here's the kicker: if you DOUBLE that number, well... you get the idea. Your savings would be exponential.

Whatever payment strategy you pick and stick with, the bottom line is that an extra payment each year or even a little extra every month could save you YEARS of debts and THOUSANDS in interest.

33. HOUSE HACKING 101

If you own a home, the basic idea here is to use other people's rent to offset (or even profit from) your own housing costs. Let someone else pay your mortgage, and leave you with the home equity! You'll begin building wealth through real estate and earning tax benefits as well.

Sounds great, but how does it work exactly? House hacking is the act of buying a place with an extra bedroom or a duplex, triplex, or quadplex with extra units. In doing so, you can rent those units out as a way as to cover the mortgage for the entire property. If done right, this cash flow from tenants also inhabiting your property could cover your monthly mortgage completely while you live there without needing to pay a dime. It might even bring in additional money monthly!

A word of caution because it is actually relatively complicated: be sure you could afford the entire mortgage with enough cash reserve before you jump in because it might take time to fill all the units or multiple units become empty at the same time in the future. Even with a lease in place, a tenant could fall behind on a payment, leaving you stuck with a large bill to cover in the meantime.

34. GO TINY

A big mistake many people make is buying too much house, tying up a huge portion of their net worth and monthly cash flow in real estate. In fact, according to Investopedia, the average single-family house has grown nearly three times in terms of square-footage from 983 in 1950 to 2,623 in 2018.

Spending beyond your needs or means can lead to becoming "house poor," meaning you're paying too much for your house and don't have enough liquidity to pay other bills or save sufficiently. Counting on a home as an investment is risky, and you should always diversify and not rely on real estate as your sole net worth. One way to own a home while still freeing up your cash flow is to go tiny.

In an article entitled "Here's how much space we waste in our big American homes, in one chart" Marketwatch highlighted how much house goes wasted. They wrote, "A research team affiliated with UCLA studied American families and where they spend most of their time while inside their homes. The results were fascinating." Here is that chart:

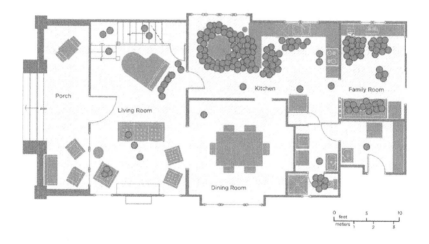

Source: MarketWatch

That's a ton of wasted space. Looks like the dining room was hardly ever used! But hey, at least they played their piano from time to time...

In late 2019, my girlfriend and I became pretty obsessed with tiny houses. Okay, obsessed might be a bit of an understatement. What started as a curious look into alternative living turned into checking out numerous library books, watching countless videos, reading blogs, listening to podcasts, and more. I'll admit, we want to buy a home but it doesn't feel realistic with student loans hanging over both of us and living in Seattle, one of the most expensive and fastest-growing real estate markets in the country. That's why we found ourselves wanting to buy a "house" we could afford. I didn't mind if it was 250 square feet and on wheels. It would be ours.

One weekend we looked at a tiny home as serious, interested buyers. The next, we rented a tiny house Airbnb about an hour north of Seattle to give it a try. I documented these weekends in a video on my YouTube channel and, of course, I highly recommend watching, especially if you have any personal interest in tiny real estate. We got so far into our research that we learned many recommend adding solar panels, especially if you're considering going totally off-grid! You can use an online calculator to see if solar panels could make sense for you. One I recommend is from EnergySage.com.

Want to check one out for yourself? We found the best way to find Tiny House rentals is to simply search "Airbnb Tiny House Lists" on Google. There are lots of websites that have updated listings to rent. A great example can be found on Dream Big Live Tiny Co.'s blog.

Here is a list of more resources I recommend if you are interested in going tiny:

- Blog | Tiny House Giant Journey
- YouTube | Living Big In A Tiny House
- Shop Tiny Houses for Sale | Tiny House Listings
- Podcast | Tiny House Lifestyle
- Website | Tiny House Forum
- Book | Tiny House: Live Small, Dream Big
- Book | Tiny House Design & Construction Guide

One final thought for your consideration: In my research, I found that many bought their tiny home with the intention of living in it for a few years while paying it off, then renting it out and utilizing it as a new source of passive income. That was a direction we were leaning. We temporarily tabled the idea because our dream two-bedroom apartment opened up in our building and we adopted a puppy BUT I imagine we'll start having tiny conversations again in the not-so-distant future.

Pro Tip: If you're a nomad or considering a tiny house travel lifestyle, join a national gym chain that is available in areas you're traveling to or living near. There's nothing like a nice, long, hot shower when you haven't had an extended one in weeks!

***

CHAPTER SIX

Food (For Thought) Hacks

According to the Washington Post, food costs have jumped 26% in the past decade. Motley Fool estimates we spend $5,339 annually on eating out, coffee, alcohol, and other nonessentials. CNBC's Make It cited a study that found 49% of millennials spend more on dining out than they put towards retirement. USA Today highlighted the fact that millennials eat out five times a week, 14% more than baby boomers. Yes, Starbucks and bar tabs count.

How can we resist with access to so many food delivery services that make ordering in and staying out of the kitchen *so easy*? Plus, you had a long day, a new episode of Survivor is about to start, and this is probably better for the environment because you'll save good clean water by not doing dishes (hint, you would be very wrong).

Tracking your purchases alone should help you identify if your food consumption costs are out of control. Are you buying coffee five days a week? Do you buy lunch daily and tip well without hesitation? Did you have one too many drinks last weekend and decide to pick up the bar tab for everyone? Tracking is a good foundational strategy to reduce one of your three biggest spending categories. But hacking is how we go beyond…

35. LEARN TO HACK IT AS A COOK

This hack has a bit of a start-up cost but it is absolutely worth it and helps you develop an essential life skill in the process. In terms of cost, you'll want to stock up on pantry essentials and kitchen tools to ensure you have a foundation for simple, balanced, low-cost dinners that you can make with low effort or chef skills. Here's a quick list of what I always keep in my kitchen, to help you get started: salt, pepper, garlic, mayonnaise, dijon mustard, soy sauce, hot sauce, honey, peanut butter, olive oil, sesame oil, vinegar, all-purpose flour, white sugar, rice, bread, tortillas, quinoa, canned tomatoes, pasta sauce, coconut milk, broth, almonds, pecans, chickpeas, black beans, spaghetti, and penne.

If you never cook, getting started with finding recipes and trying them out can seem daunting but here are some great resources I recommend:

- Videos by Tasty
- Cookbooks from the library
- Apps like Yummly, Epicurious, Allrecipes, and Food Network
- Food box subscriptions—the cheapest and tastiest I have found and used for years is Dinnerly
- Master Chef Junior for the feel-good inspiration alone!
- And of course, good ol' YouTube

> **Pro Tip**: Grow your own herbs and vegetables. Money doesn't grow on trees, but you can grow a tree that saves you money in your yard or on your patio. A couple years back we bought a $10 tomato plant from Costco that provided at least two dozen ripe tomatoes over the summer. Try making your own bread, pasta, and pickles too! Heck, don't stop there. Try making your own cleaning supplies, detergent, soap, candles—think of any common products and essentials and see if you can hack it by making it yourself!

36. STOCK UP ON BEVIES IN BULK

You might think alcohol is impulsive only at happy hours and on the weekends when you go out. However, when we create our grocery lists (if you don't create a list, please do) we generally add these common items:

-Beer

-Wine

I'm sure you already see where I'm going with this… personally, I tend to put these two items on the bottom of my list and grab these tasty adult beverages last. By the time I'm towards the end of my list I'm exhausted, ready to be home, and waiting even a second longer will *surely mean double the length of lines at the front* (my brain makes things up when it's tired from shopping). Therefore, I spend next to no time thinking about how much I need or what I'm spending. Grab and go. Don't do that. Instead, stock up—even if this means one extra trip out of your way. For example, I recommend Costco. But you could also collect coupons and take them to Bevmo or Wine World or Planet Cocktail… okay, I made that last one up but it has a nice ring to it!

Other ways to save on booze:

* Trader Joe's. My favorite 6 pack of Boatswain IPA runs just a cool $4.49. Less if you buy a 12-pack. $.75 a drink? Yes, please!
* Make your own beer and/or kombucha.
* Consider cutting back and replacing with mocktails.
* And finally, a great tip I learned from Life Hacker (and tested myself) is to save money on liquor by buying the cheapest vodka you can find and running it through a carbon water filter like a Britta two to three times. The result is vodka that tastes like the good stuff! Seriously!

Pro Tip: You probably know what I mean when I say you should never shop for groceries on an empty stomach. The same can be applied to shopping for alcohol. Never shop for alcohol when you could *really use a drink*. For example, every Friday at 5 pm. Brunch hours on a Sunday. Anytime on Monday… The hungrier we are, the more we're likely to overspend on food. The *thirstier* we are, the more we're likely to overspend on alcohol. But let's be honest, the real hack is: don't shop for alcohol after alcohol. Especially at midnight on your way home from a birthday party bar crawl from the ma and pa corner store because "nightcaps." #Amiright?

37. ORDER YOUR GROCERIES ONLINE

This is another hack that might sound counterintuitive at first glance but there are actually a few reasons ordering your groceries online can save you money in the end.

First off, it saves you from impulse buying, like the adult beverages covered previously, because you're not wandering the aisles grabbing anything that looks good. Cookies, ice cream, frozen pizzas, bags of popcorn in three flavors so you can recreate the tin you used to get around the holidays for movie night, fancy cheese, and (my guilty pleasure) peanut butter filled pretzels. See, your mouth is watering already! That list costs a fortune and possibly a whole new wardrobe in a larger size...

Another underrated benefit of ordering groceries online is it saves you time and gas. This is especially useful if you have young children, drive a gas guzzler, or don't live particularly close to an affordable grocery store. I'll admit to going to the fancy grocery store on several occasions just because it was closer and I only needed a "few things." Until I found those pretzels...

There are lots of options out there and even some that allow you to set up recurring orders as a subscription. Imperfect Produce, for example, can save you around 30% on grocery store produce and you can pick a subscription option that works best for you. Another popular option is Amazon Fresh. They recently removed fees on your grocery delivery as long as you hit a required minimum.

38. BYO FOOD

I have learned this as true: you can bring your own food to most events, such as sporting games and the movie theater. I honestly do this often. 90% of Seattle Mariners games I attend you'll see me stroll up to the gate with a $6 Jimmy John's sandwich in hand, freshly-made just 2 blocks away, or approaching the left-field entrance with my hummus, pita chips, and sliced cucumber from home. Who needs a $10 hot dog at a ballgame? The same is true of movie theaters, but one quick word of caution regarding the movies: please, for the sake of your fellow movie-goer patrons, don't bring in anything potent or stinky. Don't be that uncool guy or gal. There's a pretty embarrassing horror story here but I'll spare you the (fishy) details...

Definitely NOT a Pro Tip: I'm *not* going to tell you to take this a step further and bring your own adult beverage to public places. I would never do that. It's probably illegal. I haven't done that. Not me... nope, probably never. Not to a picnic at a nearby park with a loved one and a pet. Not a full bottle of wine in a plastic portable rum-runner to an outdoor concert. Absolutely not. Don't do that. Pay full price. $14 a glass probably. Times 3. Plus tax and tip like a responsible adult. Why am I still talking about paying full price and why you should *not* be sneaking in a bevie here and there? Nothing to see here. Moving on...

***

CHAPTER SEVEN

Transportation Hacks

According to Kelley Blue Book, the average price of a new car in the U.S. is approximately $37,000. In the last 10 years, the cost of transportation has risen by 11%. Not to mention, the average American spends $1,977 on gas each year alone according to the U.S. Energy Information Administration. Yikes.

And if that all isn't aggravating enough, I just received my registration notice yesterday and my tabs will cost me over $200 for my Vespa in 2020 in Washington state. More than most cars in the state. Outrageous. And yet, I still do not regret living with just these two wheels. In fact, let's start there...

39. GO TWO-WHEELIN'

One of the best decisions I've made in my mission to get out of debt and get good with money was ditching my car. I had been contemplating it for a year or so and then, when I least expected or wanted it, fate stepped in.

I had just moved into my own one-bedroom apartment (a big upgrade from my 350-square foot studio) and, not more then two weeks later, I discovered my car had been vandalized. In short, insurance called it a total loss and gave me a check far above the Kelley Blue Book value. I spent a third on new apartment purchases like pans and deck furniture and used the other two thirds to buy a used 2014

Vespa GTS 300. Luckily for me, it had been dropped once at low speed, meaning the side body hit the ground, and thus had scratches on one side. That reduced the price tag by at least $1,000. I slapped a Seahawks magnet on top and voila. Out of sight, out of mind.

Three years later I've ridden it roughly 1,000 miles, mostly to and from work. I've had one service for an oil change. I've spent an average of $5 a month on gas. Outside of the cost to buy used, I have easily reduced my monthly transportation bill by about $75. That's almost $1,000 a year saved on gas and maintenance. If $75 doesn't sound like a lot, you could likely double your savings if you ditch a motored two-wheeler for a bicycle plus public transportation. Do good for your wallet. Do good for the environment. And, of course, use some of that savings to buy yourself a sweet retro Vespa jacket. I haven't done that... yet!

Pro Tip: Pick up an electric scooter. For less than $1,000, this two-wheeler is likely to pay for itself within a year, especially if you live within a few miles of work, your gym, and a grocery store. The only 4-wheeler I do recommend? Rollerblades of course! Can we bring those back and make them cool again, please? Let's add autopilot to them while we're at it. Looking at you, Elon Musk.

Watch Next on YouTube: Two Cents "How Cars Keep You Poor"

40. FOUR-WHEELIN' HACKS

Many people know that as soon as you drive your shiny new car off the lot, your car loses about 10% of its value. Cars lose about 60% of their value after the first 5 years of ownership. Considering the lifespan of a new car is around 15 to 20 years, it makes the most sense to let somebody else take the hit on depreciation. The sweet spot when looking for a "new" car is to consider cars that are 5 or 6 years old. People seeking F.I.R.E. (or, "Financial Independence, Retire Early"— more in Chapter 15) recommend buying in the $5,000 range and always paying in full with cash. If you're buying a used car, ask for receipts from any maintenance that was done on the vehicle. If the seller is able to provide those, take that as a great sign that the previous owner took great care of it!

If you're buying from a dealer, never trade in your current car to bring down the price on a newer car! It's always better to sell your car independently. Dealerships want to make a profit on your trade-in so they generally offer the wholesale price, lower than what an independent buyer would pay. It takes a little extra time to sell it privately (and you probably want that cash ASAP) but it's well worth the effort.

> **Pro Tip**: If you own your car and don't drive it often, consider renting it out on Turo. Turo is a new site that allows users to rent from "trusted hosts around the world." A quick search shows me over 200 results in Seattle for an upcoming weekend starting at just $19 a day for a 2008 Toyota Camry. There are also over two dozen Teslas renting for around $100-200 a day. Don't worry. I'll add to cart, wait 48 hours, and completely forget about it...

41. FIND CHEAP GAS

If it's worth it to take some extra time and effort to earn more money, it's also very much worth it to take some extra time to save a little money. Drive a little out of your way to get lower gas prices. $.10, $.20, and sometimes as much as $.50 a gallon really adds up, especially if you have a larger tank or a long commute and you do this consistently. The question then becomes, how do you find the cheapest gas? There are actually a few quick and easy ways to do so:

- Try the free GasBuddy app.
- Search "gas prices" in Google Maps. This simple trick *works*!
- If you're a member, get gas at Costco or Sam's Club. It almost always beats other local gas prices by a long shot and is definitely worth the wait.

Another useful gas hack to remember is to keep your tires filled to the appropriate level. This could not be easier, and can improve your gas mileage by 0.6% on average and up to 3% in some cases. If you're not sure what the right level is, you can usually find it on the sticker inside your driver's side door jamb or in the owner's manual. Bonus: it's safer on the road too!

CHAPTER EIGHT

Hack The Smaller Five

According to USA Today, the average American spends almost $18,000 a year on impulse purchases and nonessentials like grooming, subscription boxes, cable, online shopping, happy hours, gym memberships, apps, and streaming services… Which is ironically just a tick under the annual maximum contribution for a 401(k)!

While a good chunk of these "nonessentials" fall into The Big Three, especially the food and transportation categories (think takeout and rideshares), a large portion falls into what I'm calling "the smaller five": travel, cell phone plans, entertainment, dating, and healthcare (even though it definitely isn't nonessential—double-negative much?—healthcare can be a huge money-suck).

Now that I think about it, "smaller" five is misleading. I should call these the *less big five but still a solid chunk of your monthly budget…*

42. TRAVEL HACKS

Traveling is one of my favorite things in life, as it is for many. I especially love traveling on the cheap and I'll admit and I'm egregious over planner. I want to fully enjoy myself without worry, even at the expense of looking like an obvious tourist due to the oversized fanny pack around my waist! Here are a handful of my favorite hacks when it comes to travel that don't require strange attire:

Know when to fly

Tuesdays and Wednesdays are the cheapest days to fly. The great people at TravelPulse.com developed an algorithm to tell you the recommended time to book your flight, depending on the season, to save the most money. If you're flying in the winter, book 94 days before your trip; spring is 84; summer is 99, and fall is 69.

Instead of booking a hotel or entire unit, consider booking a room

Sites like Airbnb allow you to book a small space in a larger house or unit, saving you hundreds. This might be a private room or even a small unit like a furnished basement with its own in and out access. This is especially wise if you're traveling alone.

Scan your passport, identification, and itinerary and email them to yourself

Be sure to download these backup documents to your phone as well in case you don't have access to the internet. This comes in handy in the event of a loss or theft. It's less handy if your phone gets lifted so also consider printing these scans out.

Tell your credit and debit card companies that you're traveling

It's no fun having your card or cards get shut off due to suspicious activity when you're traveling. I'm sure I don't need to explain this one further but a little reminder might go a long way.

Charge phones and other devices via the television's USB slot

Most modern televisions have an unused powered USB slot on the back. Use it to plug in your phone, especially if you forgot the wall charger. Or use it simply to leave the outlets free for other devices.

Stop buying souvenirs while traveling

Your BFF isn't going to keep that postcard. Your niece is going to outgrow that t-shirt. Your boss totally forgot where you went and doesn't want anything unless it's edible. Plus, now one of your coworker's feelings are hurt because they didn't get chocolate covered macadamia nuts from Hawaii. Realistically, nobody will care or notice if you don't bring presents back. You also don't need a $15 magnet or t-shirt. You still went to Cabo, even if you don't have the tank top to prove it. Stop wasting your money on overpriced tourist junk you'll toss or forget about and save your money!

> **Pro Tip:** Go beyond and consider geoarbitrage. This is the concept of comparing the cost of living between two places and choosing to relocate to the one that is cheaper while maintaining the same level of income. In doing this, you can earn money in one area and spend it in another where that money goes further. For example, people at my company in Seattle work remotely from all parts of the U.S., including many that have a much lower cost of living. They're getting that Big City Paycheck, but living a much more reasonably priced life so they're able to save and get ahead. Some even started out in Seattle but bought a house on the other side of the country because of our flexible teleworking policy.

43. CELL PHONE HACKS

In 2018, J.D. Power reported that the average monthly cell phone bill cost $157 for households. The reality is a lot of people haven't reconsidered their cell phone bill in years. Many of us don't shop around because it's an automatic charge that we just don't think much about. As a society, we tend to value convenience over cost. I get it. But, it isn't super inconvenient to save on your monthly bill. Here are 7 quick ways to do so:

Sign up for automated payments & paperless billing
Most carriers will knock $5 to $10 off your bill for doing so. If your carrier is offering this, take advantage. PLUS, now you don't have to think about it and you won't be hit with any late fees.

Update your service address
Taxes and fees that are added to your bill each month are based on where you live. So, if you've moved to a new state or someone in your

family has (and you're on a family plan), you could save big just by updating your service address.

Cash in on discounts

Are you a student, government employee, or service member? There's likely a discount for you. Do you work for a company that offers a corporate discount? Not sure? Ask! Do you bank with a credit union? You might also be eligible for a discount. Call your carrier and ask about any and all discounts they offer.

Consider a family plan

Add lines! Sure, your bill might go up overall, but splitting a family plan with other people can lower the amount you each owe each month. The best part is, they don't even have to be family. You can share a plan with your best friends, neighbors, soccer team, book club... The more the merrier, and most carriers don't ask any questions about who all these random people are.

Switch carriers

Discount carriers come at a low cost and offer the same call quality as the bigger companies because they use the same network. Often called MVNOs, these "mobile virtual network operators" buy a share of the major carrier's network and pass the savings on to you. The drawback? Some cite call quality issues and data speed caps, likely because priority is often given to the Big Four. Funny to think that people still use their pocket texting machine for phone calls!

Prepay for data and use WiFi

If you don't need an unlimited plan, pay for your data upfront for some additional savings, and keep a close eye on your usage. One way to do so is to sign up for alerts via text message if your carrier offers them. Plus, of course, use your WiFi or even public WiFi whenever possible to limit your data usage. I also recommend you limit background data usage, a setting you can change easily.

Pay for your phone in full & avoid a payment plan

Pay now, save later. This doesn't mean charging your phone on your credit card and figuring it out later. This means saving up so you can pay for your phone in full in cash. Steer clear of rolling the cost of a brand new phone and then some into your monthly bill. And while it may sound obvious, here's your obligatory reminder to consider buying used and keeping your phone longer. They are definitely designed to last more than 2 years!

44. DATING & RELATIONSHIPS HACKS

According to Match's latest Singles in America survey, "30% of the connected generation feel as though their financial stability is having an effect on their readiness to find a true relationship." Further, 21% of millennials believe they need to reach a certain income level to even pursue a relationship, versus 14% of singles overall. Which is honestly sad. First of all, you can definitely pursue love and happiness on any income and budget. And second of all, I get it. Dating IS expensive. But it doesn't have to be.

First, planning is key. Think of inexpensive, relaxing dates like grabbing a coffee, walking through a local park, watching a game at a brewery, or meeting for happy hour for cheap bites. Keep it simple and have a great back-up or two. Second, do your research. Museums typically have a free day once a month. The same is true of art walks. Zoos sometimes offer discounts on certain days of the week. Movie theaters usually offer a discount for matinee showings. And finally, communicate. Don't wait for the bill to arrive to see who blinks first. Offering to split doesn't make you look cheap or frugal. It makes you look thoughtful and smart. And who wouldn't want to date a thoughtful, smart person? Take the lead, make suggestions, and do it early. That will set the tone and allow you to focus on what's most important: good fun and good conversation.

> **Pro Tip:** Appoint a relationship CFO. I know it's not sexy but it would be smart to treat your relationship as you might a business by putting the individual best with finances in charge of all finances. This isn't for every couple but it might be essential in situations where financial opposites have attracted! Fun fact: Married people are wealthier than single people in every age group. No pressure or anything...

45. ENTERTAINMENT HACKS

Sometimes I Netflix during Netflix when Netflix goes to the Netflix.

That little piece of diction art represents how Netflix and streaming services have infiltrated society, and sometimes my Netflix of thought. And rightfully so! There's so much good Netflix on Netflix! But it's about time we fight back and take on Netflix and other entertainment of the world with our wallets and brains. Here are a few hacks to help you have your entertainment-cake and enjoy extra money too.

Cancel your favorite streaming service for a month

If said service costs you $10 a month and you decide to go without for even just 1 month, you effectively earned a 12% discount on the year! Pick two months to live without and you almost save 25% off the annual sticker price. My personal recommendation is to go a whole summer without!

Cancel dormant subscriptions

HBO. Hulu. Birch box. Blue Apron. StitchFix. Random apps you signed up for and keep getting charged for. Magazines still delivering to an old address. Take 5 minutes and cancel them all! If you're not using it, you should never pay for it.

Protect your screens & things

Many people swear by insurance for devices like cell phones. Instead, I spend $5 to $10 to order protective screens and use the old school method of treating my expensive tech devices with love and care. They (definitely don't) have feelings too!

Let loose one day a month
You're human. Allow yourself to be human and have a fun human splurge day once a month! See a 3D movie and order that extra large bag of buttered popcorn. Go see the traveling musical in town. Buy box seats to the football game. The key is to pick a day in advance and be good on ALL the other days. Delayed gratification can be a wonderful thing!

Are you not entertained? That one goes out to my finance gladiators! Plus, an obvious excuse to quote my favorite movie...

46. TRY THESE HSA HEALTH CARE HACKS

Health care costs are up 21% in the last decade (Washington Post, 2019). Yikes is right. But honestly, not surprising. In the future when you've retired and that trend continues, guess what your highest expense becomes? You guessed it: health care. I seriously wish I had all the answers here. Sadly, this is a complicated topic that would require a whole book in and of itself. But you're here for the hacks!

A Health Savings Account (HSA) is my favorite retirement account and one that most people I know aren't taking advantage of. Money goes in tax-deferred, money invested grows tax-deferred, and money can be taken out and spent tax-free on eligible medical expenses in retirement. If that last one doesn't sound like a huge perk, medical expenses are one of the highest expenses most people face in retirement. Additionally, once you reach age 65, you can use your HSA funds on *anything* on a taxable basis. On top of all that, here are two HSA hacks to make this account even sweeter:

You may make a one time transfer from your Traditional IRA or Roth IRA to your HSA.
One time does not mean annually. You can only make this type of

transfer one time *ever*. When would you consider doing this? When you are just getting started with your HSA. This is a great way to kickstart your HSA and get beyond the threshold your provider has set to invest extra funds (typically any cash over $1,000 or $2,000).

Reimbursements have no time limit.
In other words, if you pay for medical expenses out of pocket now, even though they are HSA eligible, you can pay yourself back anytime. All you need to do is remember to keep proof in the form of a receipt. That part is important to not ignore and is worth repeating. You *must* hang onto this proof, at least until you file your taxes for the year you paid yourself back. I suggest you keep this proof organized digitally. So what makes paying yourself back later such an incredible hack? It's simple: if you leave the money in the HSA and keep it invested long term, it can grow tax-free! Then, pay yourself back any time, ideally way later! You can even use this paid back money on anything, including to help with a financial hardship or as a down payment for a house.

A few final notes about HSAs: There are no income limitations when it comes to making contributions and you can contribute even without income. Meaning, even early in retirement, you can continue to contribute and grow your funds annually. Plus, the contribution limit goes up by $1,000 (from $3,550 to $4,550) once you reach age 55. Can you tell I'm a huge fan of the HSA?

Pro Tip: Lower your prescription drug costs. If you suffer from chronic illnesses or conditions, saving money here is a big deal. There are helpful, free apps to find coupons for just about every medication that you can download and use on the go. One example is GoodRX. This finds coupons for your prescription. Possibly even for free! Even if you have insurance, the deals you'll find with these apps are often lower than your copay. With these apps, you can order online or pick your prescription up in person. (Optimal Finance Daily Podcast, Episode 1104)

Source: Forbes "Take Advantage of the HSA Loophole"

PART 3

Fun & "Easy" Money Hacks

CHAPTER NINE

Income Hacks

I'll never forget the first time I heard about the guy that made a million dollars selling pixels on a web page he created. In 2005, Alex Tew, a student from WIlshire, England, created a website to help raise money for his education. He sold image-based pixels on a 1000x1000 based grid for one dollar per 10x10 block. Purchasers put any image they desired on their block and could link to anywhere. Needless to say, at the end of the day, he actually made more than one million dollars from the site when he auctioned off the last 1,000 pixels on eBay.

Clearly, when it comes to hacking your income, creativity and dedication are key. Let's get that right (Gordon Ramsay voice). But let's get something else right: opportunities are abundant in today's digital world. But not just abundant—opportunities are seemingly endless. But why should you hack your income and go beyond traditional income routes? In short, because everyone else is doing it!

In 2019, 50% of millennials had some sort of side hustle. Further, 30% of all adults engaged in gig work, according to a 2018 report from the Federal Reserve. 16% of gig workers report that their side hustles are their main source of income. It's clear that many work beyond their traditional 9 to 5 paycheck, and for good reason. Making money on the side, creating passive income, and even starting your own business has never been easier. Let's dive into each of those topics and more to help you hack the way you make your money AND hold onto more of it.

47. SIDE HUSTLE ONLINE

"There's always money in the banana stand."
-Arrested Development

The more money you have coming in, the more you can set aside to save and invest. It can cut literal months off the time it takes you to reach retirement. That's why many turn to side hustles to supplement their income by trading extra time for extra money. You've probably heard of many in-person side hustles like driving for Uber, walking dogs, or delivering groceries. But some of my favorite side hustles don't even require you to leave home! Here are 10 of my favorite side hustle ideas to help you get started with your (online) banana stand to get the (fruit) juices flowing:

- Take online surveys
- Get paid to listen to songs and provide feedback
- Become a virtual assistant or bookkeeper
- Sell things around the house on eBay or Craigslist
- Start social media channels for local businesses or run social media ads
- Teach online. Think English, music lessons, or math.
- Wrap your car with advertisements via sites like Wrapify
- Become a user tester and give website feedback
- Become a consultant using skills you have
- Transcribe interviews and/or videos

If you don't know what something is on this list but it grabbed your attention, do some research. In actuality, when you start any new endeavor, you should always do your research to set yourself up for success before just jumping in. Most side hustles require patience and creativity. It may not come easy but you can't side hustle if you don't get started.

Watch Next on YouTube: The Money Resolution "21 Ways To Make Money Online"

48. NEGOTIATE YOUR SALARY

Got a job offer? Great! A new job is one of the best ways to increase your wealth and grow it over time. However, a mistake many make is taking the first offer. And I get it, it's an exciting moment and you're ready to ditch your old gig for an upgrade. Congrats! But slow down, be grateful, and then... ask for more! This might be your best opportunity to boost your salary because, in most cases, the 2% cost of living increases and annual raises that most companies offer will barely keep up with inflation. Okay, it makes sense. But how do you do it? Here are 7 concrete steps to negotiate a new job offer, courtesy of @thepennyhoarder via Instagram:

- Do your research
- Know your worth
- Respond to the original offer
- Plan your counteroffer
- Practice the conversation
- Negotiate
- Get it in writing

First, do your research. Use sites like Glassdoor, Indeed, PayScale, or even LinkedIn to help you find what your position is worth in your market. Knowing your worth is key when it comes to negotiation.

Next, be sure you don't delay too long in responding to the offer. Thank them sincerely and ask about next steps and timing. Ideally, they will cover benefits and open the conversation up to questions. If they haven't brought up the negotiation, this is the time to ask if the offer's salary is firm or if it has wiggle room (don't say wiggle room, but you get the idea). It might feel uncomfortable but the hiring manager is extremely used to it. Some offers even come with a timeline that includes a day or two for negotiation.

When it comes to making an ask, you need to use your research to plan a counteroffer. Practice this conversation if needed. Don't be wishy-washy. Ask for a number, not a range. Meeting in the middle of your ask and their offer is perfectly acceptable. Just be sure, no matter what, that you have it in writing. If nothing else, at least you won't have any regrets because, as you likely know, you don't get what you don't ask for.

49. LABEL YOUR CREDIT CARDS

This is one of my favorite hacks and it's so simple. If you already own a label maker, this hack is totally free and will help you earn extra credit card rewards points. If you don't, you might want to "invest" in one after hearing this super simple useful hack:

Label your credit cards so you know exactly how to get the most out of each card. Certain cards give you more rewards for groceries. Others give you more for transportation. Admittedly, it can become extremely hard to keep track of all the different benefits. Even if you only have two or three cards, this hack can really come in handy and help you gain more rewards by using the right card on the right purchase. Some cards give up to 5% cash back on rotating categories. That's essentially a 5% discount you might be missing out on if you aren't organized.

I'll be honest, between trying to help bag my groceries, giving that dark chocolate display by the register the side-eye, and showing my ID for wine, I can get a little flustered at the cash register. I simply don't have time to stop and think about which piece of plastic I should be grabbing in the heat of the battle. Label your cards so you don't have to think. Be prepared before you go into the front lines of the grocery store, gas station, or online travel portal.

Pro Tip: YouTuber Dave Hansen (Hey There, Dave Here) does not recommend any credit cards with an annual fee. Talk about simple. There are tons of credit cards out there that offer awesome perks and cash back without a yearly bill. Ditch the trend and go fee-less. You can easily find the best fee-less cards for you with some quick research at www.thepointsguy.com or www.nerdwallet.com.

50. REDUCE YOUR TAXABLE INCOME

Contribute as much as you can to tax-advantaged retirement accounts like your 401(k) and IRA. For the sake of round numbers, if you make $100,000 in a year but max out your 401(k) at $19,500 (as of 2020), you'd only owe taxes as if you had earned $80,500. Another $6,000 to max out your IRA and you've reduced your taxable income roughly 25%. If you're over 50, by contributing the max for these two retirement accounts combined, you could reduce your taxable income by $33,000!

But wait, there's more! If you have a high deductible health care plan and a Health Savings Account (HSA), you could max your HSA out and reduce your taxable income by another $3,550 as an individual or by $7,100 if you have family coverage.

Here are more ideas to research, explore, and consider:

- Contribute to a 529 account (more on this in Chapter 16)
- Deduct business expenses you're entitled to
- Deduct qualifying educational expenses, even if you're not working towards a degree
- Deduct mortgage interest and property taxes
- Make energy-efficient improvements to your home like solar panels
- Take advantage of tax-loss harvesting
- While possibly extreme, move to a state with lower taxes

51. BECOME A COMPANY OF ONE

In 2019, I read Paul Jarvis's book "Company of One" and it completely validated so many thoughts that had been floating around my noggin. On his podcast, Paul Jarvis explains, "The bigger your business gets, the more work it requires, and it may not be the work you enjoy. Working for yourself is freedom if you do it right... Question if more is actually better. The opposite approach of most startups or corporations. More does not equal better. Sometimes *enough* equals better." He explains why going small is the next big thing. A trendy term for this is to become a "solopreneur."

I'll admit, I'm a bit of a control freak. I have tons of ideas (must write down, must organize, must share as a book) so being my own boss would give me freedom and total control. No one to rely on. No one to blame. No one to help. But also, no one else to pay. Simplicity. Produce, earn, and keep.

A company of one can start simple. For me, it was a self-published book, "The Money Resolution". That turned into social channels, a website, and a blog—all of which I hope to monetize in the future. I learned about affiliate links and incorporated those. I claimed the name on YouTube. *This won't turn into a long-term commitment, right?* After a few videos, I was totally hooked and that became my new focus. So much so, this new book was supposed to be out a year ago! Sharing videos on YouTube led to working on a course. Which led to wanting to start a podcast while self-quarantining during the Coronavirus outbreak of early 2020. Let's fire up a Patreon for my most loyal supporters (all 3 of them!). I fought those urges but continued to scale what was working and what I was enjoying slowly. *Gradually then suddenly* I hoped and reminded myself.

The whole idea behind my first book and now brand "The Money Resolution" is to build different streams of income that all feed into one another. While outside help would be refreshing (and honestly much needed from time to time), there is something so satisfying about doing it all on your own from the ground up and, someday, possibly, reaping all the rewards for it. That's not the goal with my brand but it's the challenge and the destination I'm driving towards. I may look back years from now and cringe at this very section but at least I'll look back with satisfaction knowing everything I wrote, every video on YouTube, every good and bad idea was mine.

With a little traction and a solid foundation, I have big personal goals for "The Money Resolution". I'm aiming high but will keep the business small and nimble. But the idea here is to build a brand and gradually build upon it.

If you're just getting started, start small and stay small. Do what you love, not what you think you're supposed to do. Learn, try, fail, repeat. When you're willing and able, expand. Monetize. Grow. You'll learn so much about business, life, and (if you pay attention) yourself.

What could this look like for you? Pursue a side hustle. Write that book you've dreamed of writing. Start that Etsy store. Put together your favorite personal recipes and sell them as a PDF online. Become a consultant if you have a unique skill others could use. One of these ideas and efforts may become a hobby, then a passion, then a business. If you're lucky and work hard enough, maybe one day you can walk away from your nine-to-five and work towards making *yourself* rich, not somebody else.

52. CREATE A PATH TO PASSIVE INCOME

"If you don't find a way to make money while you sleep,
you will work until you die."
-Warren G. Buffet

Passive income. The holy grail of income. Make money while you sleep. It's the dream, isn't it? (I'm aware of the pun). I remember the first time I learned about passive income years ago...

Our beer league softball team decided to grab a drink after a game in the Queen Anne neighborhood of Seattle. I struck a conversation up with a stranger and at some point we asked each other what the other does for a living. My story was lame. Her story blew my mind. She told me she makes something called "passive income" selling ringtones online. "But really, I don't work because I don't have to."

record scratch sound

Hold up, what? I thought to myself.

"Drinks on you?!" fell out of my mouth as I stood there stunned. She went on to explain to me that's what I need to be looking for—an opportunity to make money without having to exchange time for money. For a few years, I asked around and searched for ideas. I failed at many. I didn't actually get it and it felt elusive. No, impossible.

Otherwise, EVERYONE would be doing it, right?

Seven years later I published my first book and after my first $150 or so direct deposit check from Amazon, I was hooked. That's a synonym for addicted, right? My only regret: I ignored a very bright light for so many years. The topic of passive income could be a whole book in and of itself but you're here for hacks so here are 15 ways you can make money while you sleep with one very important disclaimer at the end. Actually two.

- Self-publish a book via Kindle Direct Publishing. Hint: it doesn't have to be long. It can even be a notebook or book of pretty quotes or charts.
- Join the Amazon Affiliate program if you have a website or any sort of social media following.
- Create a digital product like a workbook or planner and sell it on Etsy as a download.
- Create and sell stock photography.
- Create and sell an online course.
- Start and monetize a YouTube channel. You need 1,000 subscribers and 4,000 watch hours over the course of a year to generate income via Google AdSense revenue.
- Start a blog or website and sell ads.
- Create a game or invention. Consider getting it funded on Kickstarter.
- Become an Amazon Audible narrator via Audiobook Creation Exchange.
- Create other digital products like ringtones, music for videos, wallpapers, cinematic video editing LUT packs, and more.
- Create and sell digital templates, logos or designs.
- Start a podcast and find sponsors to support it.
- Rent out your car using the site Turo.
- Rent out parking spots or extra space in your house as storage using the site Neighbor.
- Create and sell a niche website based on trending topics. Example: best avocado recipes for millennials. Joking. Or am I?

Disclaimer #1:

You CANNOT create passive income without hard work and/or money upfront. You have to be willing to put in the time and effort. None of these ideas are guaranteed to succeed. My first book made very little in profit and was a LOT of work. Do your research. Plan. Take your time. Find mentors to help guide you. Dedicate yourself. And then, and only then, it MIGHT work out.

Disclaimer #2:

As soon as you start to earn passive income you'll likely dream of retiring early on a beach, sipping margaritas. You might get there, but it's very unlikely. You'll probably become addicted. You'll continue to work and strive for more passive income like a drug. However, for once, it will be because you want to. You'll find ways to help people, make a difference, and do what you love instead of punching in and out of a 9 to 5 job. Let me be clear: THIS is the dream. THIS is the passive income goal. THIS is why we hack.

Watch Next on YouTube: The Money Resolution "Passive Income Ideas: 10 Ways To Earn Money While You Sleep"

CHAPTER TEN

Spending Hacks

It might sound unbelievable, but even most millionaires still seek out deals and don't eat fancy meals at restaurants often. Chris Hogan, author of "Everyday Millionaires", explains that 93% of millionaires use coupons when shopping. 85% of millionaires still use a shopping list when buying groceries and the typical millionaire spends less than $200 on eating out at restaurants a month. They have plenty of money and yet, they are responsible frugal shoppers and spenders.

Don't worry, I'm not here to tell you NOT to spend money. I'm here to explain a few creative ways you can be smart with your money and avoid buyer's remorse. Because *if spend you will, spend wise you must* (Yoda voice)...

For example, as a general rule, you should never spend more than 2 to 3 percent of your total net worth on any single purchase. Let's dig into more generic rules of thumb when it comes to spending your money wisely. Of course I'm kidding. Let's hack our spending and have fun doing it!

53. ONLINE SHOPPING HACKS

Raise your hand if this statement applies to you: I spend more money online than I do in stores. My guilty hand is also in the air. BUT the reality is, that's the new normal so I'm not here to finger wag. I totally get it. It's convenient. Not to mention the online ads that literally follow us around the internet like peer pressure bullying us to buy and dozens of deals hitting our inbox daily. Who can resist a solid BOGO deal that ends tonight at midnight?! Plus, almost everything ships free!

You earned that disposable income so by all means, dispose of it (sounds weird when you say it that way, right?). Let's get creative and make that spending go further. Here are a few of my favorite ways to save while shopping online:

Install and use the browser plugin Honey

What's a plugin? A plugin is essentially an app for your web explorer. When Honey is installed, it will automatically look for discount codes and apply the best one to your shopping cart. It's as simple as that. Honey is even more powerful on Amazon, where it will show you the price history and allow you to set up a "Droplist" so that you can be notified if the item you're looking for drops below a certain threshold. Pretty sweet, right? Just don't forget to spread the love and share your codes when checking out as well, if Honey prompts you to do so.

Choose no-rush shipping whenever possible

Not only is it good for the environment because all of your items will ship together in one box but, as of this writing, you can earn $5 on your Amazon Prime Now account or credit towards Prime Video rentals when you choose no-rush shipping. Win-win!

Sell your gift cards

If you have a pile of gift cards stacking up in a shoebox that you're not going to spend, go to www.GiftCardGranny.com OR www.raise.com and sell yours for cash! Sure, you won't get the full value back but any cash is better than an unused piece of plastic gathering dust. This is also a great place to pick up gift cards at a discount at places where you shop often. Another win-win!

Shop on Tuesdays and Fridays

Believe it or not, there are days of the week that offer better deals online. Studies have shown that discounts are highest on Tuesdays, followed by Fridays. The worst days to shop? The weekend. The worst months to shop online? March and August. I just have to wonder if this was actually an addiction masked by a "study". Either way, good to know!

Watch Next on YouTube: The Money Resolution "Here's the BEST way to save money on AMAZON (use Honey)"

54. USE THE 30/30 SHOPPING RULE

I learned this one from The Minimalists Podcast. They explained a super useful shopping tip they call the "30/30 Shopping Rule". Its genius-ness (is that a word?) is in its simplicity. It works like this: If you're considering a purchase over $30, wait 30 hours. This pause helps you think about how much you really need the item. Plus, the time away can allow you to research and find a better deal or discount elsewhere.

Taking this idea further, they explain that if you're considering a purchase over $100, you need to wait 30 days. This might sound unreasonable at first, but consider this: how often do you want to make a splurge purchase over $100 the very day you get paid? This 30-day self-check and wait time can help you pause to remember your *why*, your big goals, and what else you could do with the money. Do you really need this thing? Or is this money in your checking account just burning a hole in your pocket?? Stop. Breathe. Think. Move on. The good ol' SBTMo! (I was really hoping that would be a cool acronym I could coin, but alas).

You might be thinking, *what about purchases under $30?* Well, you're a grown-up. I simply <u>trust</u> that you'll make the right decision… said with stern eyes and a furrowed brow. Maybe they should call it the "Dad-like guilt-trip under 30" rule! Good ol' DGTU-30. Still doesn't work…

55. SEASONAL SHOPPING HACKS

This is your ULTIMATE guide to big purchases—AKA the best time to buy anything. If you would rather watch this section, check out the video on the YouTube channel. But here are the short version hacks for the optimal time to buy common big-ticket items:

Plane Tickets: *Early December, Late January-Early February*
These are the two dead times of the year. Aim to fly two weeks after Thanksgiving but well before Christmas. Winter months also mean slower travel even after the holiday season.

Engagement Rings: *Summer*
Hopefully a singular purchase… Summer is the most common time to get married, thus the cheapest time to buy! Thanksgiving through Valentine's Day is the most expensive time of year because these are the most common times for proposals.

Gym Membership & Gym Equipment: *January, Early Summer*
Contrary to others on this list, the time to join a gym or buy equipment is when people are most likely to want to work out because everyone is fighting for business.

Laptop: *April*
April is the end of the fiscal manufacturing year in Japan. Therefore, the inventory needs to be loaded off quickly. Discounts on last year's model usually run around 20% off.

Television: *Black Friday, January*
On Black Friday, you can find TVs up to half off what they normally go for. Missed Black Friday? Don't fret. Cyber Monday and Cyber Week offer excellent deals too. Plus, in January, older models still left from the Holidays need to be moved to make room for new models so pick one up for the football playoffs!

Mattress: *President's Day, Memorial Day, Labor Day*
These are best to buy during three-day weekends. Plus, it's a nice time

to shop in general because you have an extra day to sleep in and feel extra rested. That's not a thing... Fun fact: rumor has it, George Washington and Abe Lincoln were poor sleepers. Thus, Presidents' Day savings on mattresses! Also probably not a thing...

Large Appliances: *May, September, October*
In September, manufacturers debut the new washers, dryers, and dishwashers. Thus, once again, older models are marked down to make room on the sales floor. Refrigerators are a strange exception. Those debut in the spring. You might be able to save extra on refrigerators for Mother's Day and Memorial Day sales too.

Furniture: *January*
New models arrive in February so last year's models go on sale post-holidays. August was also suggested through research due to new models. Another tip: inquire about extra discounts if you're willing to shop the floor model.

New Cars: *December*
To be clear, I never recommend buying new cars. So here is a tip you can share with your rich aunt or uncle... New models arrive in September and October. Therefore, anytime in the fourth quarter of the year is a good time to shop. During these months you'll save an average of 6.1%. Because of the steep price tag, this could be 4-figure savings. September is another good month. You get the end of the third quarter of the year discounts with new models coming in and salespeople needing to hit their quarterly goals.

House: *October*
Studies have shown, houses purchased in October are 2.6% less expensive than other months. And actually, October 8th was the very best day, which was 10%+ cheaper. Strange, right? Generally speaking, the fall is a slow time. Through research, it seems anytime between August and December is a good time to buy.

56. USE YOUR HSA & FSA ON AMAZON

Let's keep this one simple because it is. However, so few people know about it. You can, quite easily without hoops, use your HSA (Health Savings Account) or FSA (Flexible Spending Account) on eligible medical expenses on Amazon. What's eligible? Well, rather than finding the list and hoping for the best at checkout, Amazon has made it super easy by providing a store to shop eligible expenses.

It's so simple to get your sunscreen, first aid kit, lip balm, breast pumps (not sure why that would be plural but also not asking), walking canes... you name it! Plus, and here's the best part, Amazon is often less expensive than common brick and mortar local pharmacies when it comes to common medical supplies.

Use your tax-advantaged funds on eligible products quickly and easily at Amazon at a better cost with super quick shipping. Brilliant!

Watch Next on YouTube: The Money Resolution "How To: Use Your FSA & HSA on Amazon"

57. JOIN THE CLUB

Club Memberships are worth it! I'm talking about Sam's Club and Costco. For example, Costco is just a $60 annual fee for the base membership (no, you don't need the Executive one), plus you can split that with a member of your household or friend if they are over 18 years of age. Even if you only shop a couple of times a year to stock up on essentials, $30 for access to amazing prices (and cheap gas) will likely more than pay for itself.

I did some pretty extensive research about 30 Costco Hacks for a Money Resolution YouTube video. Here is a sample of that list but be sure to check out the video for all 30!

- The best times to shop are 3-5 pm, Monday through Thursday.
- Rent a car at a great value through Costco online.
- Keep an eye out for deals on memberships via coupon sites

like Groupon and LivingSocial.

- Prices ending in .88 and .00 mean the store staff is trying to move it off the floor quickly. An asterisk on an item's price tag means it has hit its lowest price and won't get restocked.
- If you're buying technology and/or appliances you get free technical support AND it extends the warranty to 2 years. Elsewhere, most items come with only a 1-year warranty.
- You can use Costco cash cards to get in and shop without a membership.
- Gift card bundles like movies and restaurants are perfect for breaking up and gifting.
- Get your ink refilled for cheap, for as little as $7.49!
- Take advantage of memberships savings if you're a student or military member or veteran.
- Access your Costco membership via the app if you forgot or lost your card.
- You can return your membership. You read that right.
- Price adjustment after the fact is no issue. Don't hesitate to ask.
- Get Costco prices elsewhere. Target and Kohls will price match in most cases.
- Meat prices are a great deal and good quality. Freeze extras you're not ready to use.
- Avoid tempting aisles and sections like the center of the store where they have their most tantalizing deals.
- They ring a bell when a fresh batch of rotisserie chicken is coming out. It's just $4.99!
- And most importantly: order extra caesar sauce with your chicken bake and use it on the side as a dip.

Now you can shop at Costco like a pro. Membership is a great purchase and one that pays for itself in toilet paper, paper towels, tissues, dishwasher soap, detergent, dog food and treats, beer, and wine alone. I may or may not have gone to Costco within the last couple of days of writing this… I may or may not miss it already…

58. TAKE ADVANTAGE OF THE SALES TAX HOLIDAY

You can't escape the heat, but you can escape taxes! For one day in several states at least... According to Kiplinger Magazine, there are 17 states that offer a daylong break from paying sales tax during the summer.

This could lead to savings of 4% or more. For example, you can save 7% in states like Tennessee and even 10% in my home state of Washington! The date of this holiday varies by state, and the eligible products vary as well. Typically the date falls on a weekend over the summer but lasts as long as a week in certain states. In many cases, this tax relief applies to back-to-school shopping, hunting supplies, appliances, and household products.

Fortunately, Amazon and Walmart will honor the tax holidays online as well! With a little bit of extra time and research, you could save yourself money on purchases that you already make annually during the summer..

Alternatively, if you're close to a state without sales tax (in 2020 those are Alaska, Delaware, Montana, New Hampshire, and Oregon) you could shop online and ship your products to a friend or family member in that state. Simply drive to pick up your purchase or have them drop it off if they are already traveling near you.

59. "ALEXA, SAVE ME MONEY!"

I love home tech. I still have my original Amazon Echo and use it daily to turn lights on and off, set timers while cooking, and check what time the local sports games start. Recently, I had an idea and conducted an experiment that worked out well for the most part. I wondered, could Echo pay for itself by helping you save money and time? The short answer is yes. Here are the things Alexa can help you accomplish:

- Find quick, affordable dinner recipes
- Set reminders for things like paying bills or going grocery

shopping
- Give recommendations for a finance podcast
- Learn about the cost of living by state, including average electricity bills and gas prices
- Check-in on the stock market or… sigh… Bitcoin
- Ask for definitions for finance terms or phrases
- Make a donation to a charity
- Listen to your personal finance books through Audible
- Play a news brief with financial news
- Play reviews of purchases you're researching
- Remind yourself to do something when you get somewhere (like get milk at the grocery store)
- And just for fun… play *Who Wants To Be A Millionaire?*

Smart home technology is just getting smarter and I was very impressed by the Echo in my experiment. I honestly feel like I'm just scratching the surface with what the Echo and other home devices can do. I'm excited to see what skills and finance jokes are coming soon. Speaking of money jokes, just say "Alexa, tell me a money joke!"

> **Pro Tip**: Set up all your home smart lights to turn green when you say "Alexa, show me the money." Further proof that I truly am a personal finance nerd...

60. GOING OUT HACKS

Let me get this out of the way: fun = good. I fully support you living your life. If you're not having fun, you're not doing it right. BUT waking up trying to figure how bad the damage was is never fun. Especially when you're hungover… so here are two quick going out hacks that both support the theory "cash is king."

First, bring only cash and your ID. Sounds downright dangerous, right? What if you RUN OUT of money? Well, my friend, that means it's time to take it easy or go home. This forces you to think ahead and set a plan with your fun money budget. You'll think twice before ordering that fancy cocktail and stick to reasonable beers.

Second, keep larger bills in your pocket. Seems counterintuitive, right? Actually, studies have shown you're less likely to spend larger bills as you "splurge" the night away. Meanwhile, Swipey McSwipeRight is in the corner running up their credit card tab without noticing. So. Much. Swiping!

61. GET A CASH BACK CREDIT CARD

I've previously explained why I'm a big fan of travel rewards credit cards and listed some of my favorites. Yet still, a cash back credit card is a staple in the credit card world, and one solid cash back card belongs in almost every wallet because cash is king after all. You should always research to find the current best card for your needs and purposes but here are my favorite cash back cards I recommend as of early 2020:

Discover it Secured
This is the best card to get if you have low or no credit and you're just starting out in the rewards game. The good thing about this credit card is that they'll give you 2% cash back at gas stations and restaurants and 1% back on everything else. The best part? No annual fee!

Citi Double Cash
This card gives you a whopping 2% cash back on ALL purchases. You get 1% when you make a purchase, and then another 1% back when you pay it off. While it doesn't offer a signup bonus, my favorite thing about this card is its simplicity. You get 2% cash back on every purchase everyday. It's simple without an annual fee. Win-win! As a money minimalist, this card is my pick.

Chase Freedom
For signing up, they'll give you $150 back after you spend $500 on the card within the first 3 months. They also offer 5% cash back on revolving categories up to $1,500, as well as 1% cash back on

everything else. If you have a lot of spending it's not quite as good as the Citi Double Cash rewards card, but the $150 sign up bonus definitely makes it worthwhile, especially at first. Plus again, you get it with no annual fee.

Capital One Saver Cash Rewards
This card does come with a $95 annual fee but it also doubles the Chase signup bonus. You get $300 back after you spend $3,000 within the first 3 months. Plus, you get 4% cash back on all dining and entertainment, 2% back at the grocery store, and 1% back on everything else.

Blue Cash Preferred Card from American Express
Although there is a $95 annual fee for this card as well, you get a great welcome bonus with a $250 statement credit after you spend $1,000 in the first 3 months. You get 6% cash back at US supermarkets, 6% cash back on streaming services, 3% back on all transit, 3% back at gas stations, and 1% cash back on everything else. Did somebody say SIX percent?!

This list is just scratching the surface of the world of cash back credit cards. As a reminder, these programs change often so always do your research when picking one (you probably only need one) and always open new credit judiciously.

Pro Tip: As a general rule, remember to never buy a depreciating asset with a credit card, especially if you're not in a position to pay it off in full each month. A depreciating asset is anything you buy that loses value over time.

Watch Next on YouTube: The Money Resolution "Top Cash Back Credit Cards 2020 (with no annual fee!)"

CHAPTER ELEVEN
Free, Yes Free(!), Hacks

"There's no such thing as free."
-Roger, my stepdad

I remember a conversation with my stepdad Roger when I was 8 that started out with that above sentence. I fought tooth and nail to convince him he was wrong. But alas, he was able to poke a hole in all of my arguments and win the debate. And trust me, 8-year-olds never give up! Yet, he was convincing. Everything *does* cost time, information, or trade off of sorts.

Flash forward to present day. I open an email and see an offer for two FREE tacos at Taco Time for National Taco Day. Every time I come across something free in life, I skeptically remember what Roger told me. I read the fine print: *using a mobile app and credit card, dine-in only.* So… not free, since it costs time and information. Damn!

While Roger was mostly right, I have come to learn that there actually are plenty of great things in life that are indeed, truly free. And sometimes, free plus your time can be fun and rewarding. So, this chapter is dedicated to all the best ACTUALLY free things that save you a little cash, earn you a little cash, and let you have a little fun on the free. For example, Thrillist put together an article highlighting 98 restaurants offering free foods on your birthday!

62. TAKE ADVANTAGE OF WORK PERKS

To be clear, this doesn't read as "take advantage of work." I'm not telling you to take home reams of paper and a red stapler and commit time theft because *you deserve it*. No, no. Instead, I mean perks that are actual and legitimate opportunities for you to save.

The obvious example is an employee discount. I work at a company that sells coffee and more. I love coffee—which is an understatement. Working there was not a total accident! Previously, I worked in the jewelry business and, while I do not personally like jewelry, I did take advantage of my discount for affordable gifts when it came to birthdays and holidays.

Another example is if your company is one of those fancy start-ups that provides food, snacks, and drinks (sometimes even beer). Save money on your meal planning and save yourself time! Obviously don't be "that guy" that brings growlers and Tupperware to take things home, but take advantage of the perk at work and enjoy that free food.

There might be more unique work perks at your job that you aren't taking advantage of that can improve your financial life. Perhaps your work has a stipend for transportation, gym access, free courses or education, unused store credit, and paid-time off you're at risk of losing.

Pro Tip: Take advantage of *others'* work perks. Oftentimes, companies have some sort of friends and family discount that you might be able to take advantage of. A friend or family member might get some kind of new customer bonus they are willing to split with you. Or, they may have (legal) insider information they can share that can save you money. For example, maybe rates are dropping soon or a sale "might be on the horizon" for the thing you are looking for. I'm dancing around the topic but you get the point. It doesn't hurt to ask!

---

63. TAKE ADVANTAGE OF THE SAVER'S CREDIT

Save a little money, get a little money? Well, kind of!! Did you know:

the government will pay you, in the form of a tax credit, for saving towards retirement come tax season? So long as you:

- Are over 18 years old
- Are not a full-time student
- Are not claimed as a dependent on another person's tax return

The Saver's Credit is worth up to $1,000, or $2,000 if you are married filing jointly, and depends on the amount you have saved towards your retirement account. The federal government offsets a percentage (up to 50%) of the first $2,000 ($4,000 if married filing jointly) that you put into your 401(k), IRA, or similar tax-advantaged retirement plan. The size of the percentage depends on your adjusted gross income (AGI) for the year. In 2020, if your income does not exceed $19,500 you are eligible to get the full 50% credit as a single taxpayer. If you're the head of your household, that income limit bumps up to $29,250.

Source: NerdWallet "How the Saver's Credit Works"

64. CHURN BABY, CHURN!

Churning, like butter, can be complicated and messy but when done right is... delicious! Okay, that didn't quite track. Basically, credit card churning is the strategy of opening cards specifically to take advantage of their introductory bonuses and rewards. It's definitely advanced and you must consider any adverse effects, like damaging your credit. While it might not be for everyone, it's definitely a hack to consider!

Similar to credit card churning, bank account churning is the idea of taking advantage of new account offers. Chase, for example, recently offered $200 if you signed up for a new checking and savings account. However, be sure to read the fine print. In most cases, you will need to leave a certain amount in that account for a set number of days, for example, a $1,000 balance minimum for 90 days, to earn the cash reward.

65. FREE & FUN HACKS

Admittedly, the bulk of what I had planned to write here doesn't feel right anymore, as I'm personally two months into self-quarantining due to the Coronavirus pandemic. This has given a new meaning and appreciation for having fun indoors for free. I have been extremely inspired by the generosity and support of so many that offered free resources. Many removed paywalls, extended free trials and made their entertainment or information totally free. It's amazing how much we have bonded together globally and I'm certain there will be permanent good that comes from the ashes of this current chaos. This is tragically sad but it has brought out so much good in humanity and shown how truly resilient we are.

The COVID-19 pandemic is a deeply upsetting, unique experience —one I desperately wish we all didn't have to go through. However, through it all, it has been an incredible lesson in gratitude, creativity, resourcefulness, and charity. It brought homes and communities closer together. Plus, it brought us "Some Good News" by John Krasinski. After going through this, I don't think I will ever look to my partner and say "I'm bored" again. Pandemic aside, this is the greatest time to be alive and I've never been more grateful for the simplest things. So be alive (creatively and affordably)!

With that said, here's a quick list of things we've been doing indoors that are free, fun and awesome:

- We drew with ink and brought these drawings to life with watercolors.
- We learned how to make our own hand sanitizer. If only we could make our own toilet paper...
- We toured monuments and parks for free online because Google.
- We learned how to brew our own beer and make beer bread.
- We watched free "live" concerts on YouTube and our seats were front row!
- We learned how to hack haircuts at home.

- We play-tested a card game I invented called "Five Star Recruit." It was bad. It was fun! (Because only I understood the rules and thus, I won)

Here are a few of my original hacks for this section that make sense when things are back to our new normal:

Museum Day
Did you know there is an annual National Museum Day hosted by the Smithsonian? Participating locations offer free admission to popular museums and cultural institutions. In Washington state alone, there were seven free options throughout the Pacific Northwest last year including the Seattle Art Museum, Bellevue Arts Museum, and Tacoma Art Museum.

Try (Don't Buy) Board Games
You can try out games before you buy, by playing for free at a local board game shop. Or, meet up with friends and ask everyone to bring their favorite card or board game. This has helped us make an informed decision about the games we want to buy (or avoid wasting money on) because, when it comes to buying unplayed games, reviews online aren't dependable because we all have personal preferences when it comes to gaming types and mechanics.

The Library
You can't forget the library! The ultimate fun and free hack. A free membership gives you access to seemingly limitless books, movies, music, and more. Not to mention, many libraries host community events and can be a great place to meet your neighbors and have good, free, fun.

Pro Tip: This is more about productivity than FUN, but your local library is also a free space you can use to GSD away from the distractions of home. Most even have rooms you can reserve for some quiet time and elbow space. I find the library to be a great alternative to coffee shops that tempt me with scents of delicious scone$, muffin$, and latte$.

***

CHAPTER TWELVE

Five Quick Hacks To Help You Stack

This chapter could also be titled "The Cutting Room Floor." Outlines are necessary when approaching a book like this. However, inevitably, there's good information I want to share that doesn't fit neatly into a broader topic. That's okay. I'll just dump it all into a chapter tucked away in the middle of the book with a catchy title and nobody will notice. Unless I tell them. Whoops. Whatever. Here we go, in no particular order, I present five quick and very useful money hacks.

66. TAKE A MONEY HEALTH DAY

As I hope you know, taking a mental health day here and there is amazing and allows you to reset and catch up on rest. While we all know this to be true, very few of us take the time to schedule it. Start there. Furthermore, plan a day to take off from your job but to still "work" a full day on your personal finances instead. I would recommend taking your money health day twice a year or half a day every quarter. Put it on the calendar. Call out. Use sick time off. Use vacation. The point is, take time for you and use that time wisely to work on your finances even if you're not making money that day.

So, what exactly could a money health day look like? Well, as previously stated, look at it as an average workday. Wake up with an alarm set at your normal time. Shower and put on human, adult clothes as normal (hopefully). Then, sit at the computer and create a list. Some super quick ideas to consider are:

- Review your net worth
- Create a plan to increase your emergency fund, including projections
- Determine if fees are eating away at your nest egg and make a plan to reduce them (more on this in Chapter 13)
- Update or add beneficiaries on all of your accounts
- On that same, morbid thought... create a will at www.legalzoom.com, starting at just $89.
- Consolidate your student loans or transfer your credit card debt to a no-interest card to create a payoff strategy
- Start a project that will lead to generating passive income
- Find a way to give and budget for charitable donations, monetarily or through volunteering
- Reassess your financial goals for the year and adjust as necessary
- Tackle the to-do's you've created from this book
- Reflect on your journey and relationship with money and write about it. Who knows, maybe it'll lead to starting your own blog, podcast, YouTube channel, or book!

67. GET PET INSURANCE

According to one study by the Animal Health Institute, owners spend $9K to $13K for medical treatments over their pets' lifetimes, with only 2% having pet insurance. Treatments for one illness alone could easily cost $4K to $14K. I can attest to this...

Most pet insurance providers will provide you with a quote. It's important to shop around just like you should for home or car insurance. The average cost of pet insurance varies widely. Monthly premiums start as low as $10, but they can cost $100 and up on the high end, depending on the age and health of your pet. On average, expect to pay between $30 and $50 a month. Yes, that's $360 to $600 a year per pet, but you'll thank yourself if you experience a severe illness or life-threatening condition that requires surgery or ongoing treatment.

According to reviews.com, the five "best" pet insurance companies are:

- Figo (best for discounts)
- Healthy Paws (best for overall value)
- Trupanion (best for young and purebred pets)
- Nationwide (best for a wide range of pet species)
- PetPlan (best for young puppies and kittens, my choice for my personal preferences)

While this hack only applies to pet owners, I had to include it. I suffered a $7,000 setback while writing this book because of a pet emergency I previously mentioned. I wasn't prepared emotionally because, well, no-one can be. But I also wasn't prepared financially. Pet insurance is the only thing that might have softened the devastating blow with the loss of our family member. My pup was an angel and it was worth every penny to try to help him in his last days. But having to make financial decisions while mourning his loss was gut-wrenching, to say the least.

Source: NerdWallet "Pet Insurance Can Be Your Wallet's Best Friend" Watch Next on YouTube: The Money Resolution "Pet Insurance: What it costs, what it covers, & how to find the best"

68. TAKE A BEAT AND HIT PAUSE

"Whenever I'm about to do something I think, 'Would an idiot do that?' And if they would, I do not do that thing."
-Dwight Schrute

Here's how to deal with financial emergencies.

No, not a family crisis, a sick dog, a car accident, a loss of a job, or a broken arm. Of course, you should be prepared for those emergencies with insurance and an emergency fund.

However, I want to illustrate to you that financial emergencies come in the small variety as well. It's the little, often unexpected things that come up on a regular basis like being overdue for an oil change, grabbing happy hour after bumping into a friend, or even running out of household essentials like paper towels and deodorant. It's also the large decisions you have to make like attending an out-of-town wedding, paying for a random movie plus soda plus popcorn plus parking for a friend's birthday, or splurging on an Uber to an event because you might want to have a few drinks.

These, on the surface, don't sound like emergencies. In fact, they're not. Some of these might even sound like good problems to have. However, they can feel like *financial* emergencies. Not necessarily in the moment but after the fact when you review your credit card statement or bank account. They are drainers. They are distractions from your goals. Regret is a jerk of a friend, especially when the rent or mortgage payment is due...

But you know what? That's okay. As long as you do this: Ask yourself: "Is this worth it?" It's a simple pause. It's a simple check. It's a simple second you take to think about your why and your goals. It might be a literal second. But even if it's just that, it's not this: impulsive. There's nothing I can do to help you with everyday decisions except to remind you that you have goals and a why.

Not all spending is bad spending. Not thinking about spending is bad spending.

69. AVOID THE ENDOWMENT EFFECT

We tend to put more value on the things we already have in our possession. It's irrational and full of emotional bias but we do it anyways. This is the endowment effect. Plus, studies have shown it holds true regardless if you paid for the item or were gifted it. If you have something of value that you've held onto for a while, consider selling it by looking at it from a different perspective. I'll illustrate with an example that definitely isn't personal...

Let's say you (again, not me) had a signed Ken Griffey Jr. rookie card. You may have looked at this as an heirloom you plan to hand down to your kid one day. Maybe it'll pay for *his* kid's college? Here's the problem, baseball card value has dramatically decreased over time. Let's say it was once worth $5,000 but is now only worth $2,000. You shouldn't sell it right?

Actually, try this trick out: if you saw that same exact signed card on a shelf in a store, would you buy it? If not, sell! This works with most things you deem valuable in your possession like stocks you inherited, a fancy case of wine, vintage pogs, beanie babies, and the framed picture you have with Johnny Depp. Okay, don't sell the last one, but sell the rest! THEN do something smart with that money like put it towards credit card or student loan debt. Or invest with the strategies discussed in Chapter 14. Now that's a homerun idea! Did I strike out with that pun? Okay, onto the next hack. Batter up!

70. AVOID THE DIDEROT EFFECT

"It's amazing how fast a million dollars goes."
-Contestant Ben Driebergen during Survivor Season 40 (Winners at War)

Denis Diderot, the famous French philosopher, lived most of his life with very little to his name. In 1765, at 52-years-old, that changed almost overnight when he sold his library of encyclopedias he co-founded for $50,000 in today's US dollars. Shortly thereafter, he bought a new scarlet robe. Then everything changed.

With new money burning a hole in his pocket, he also purchased an extravagant new rug, then a fancy mirror, and a new leather chair. At that point he decided he had to redecorate his entire house. As soon as he had a few nice things, he needed more nice things to match his nice things. These reactive purchases are known as the Diderot Effect.

As we buy new things, it can create a "spiral of consumption". We think we need more and more to remain happy, when the reality is, we were happy before this new money and new stuff. The more we earn, the better we become at spending our money. That is why lottery winners sometimes end up filing for bankruptcy. That is why your holiday bonus check disappears in less than a week. This is what we must avoid.

Sometimes it even happens on a small scale, but can escalate quickly:

You join a new gym. You buy new gym clothes. New running shoes. New crossfit shoes. New sweat-proof headphones. A new wearable fitness tracker. And so on.

You invest in a new personal laptop. You buy a new keyboard and mouse. You buy a new monitor. You buy a new desk to put everything on. You upgrade to a two-bedroom apartment so you can have an office. You paint an accent wall a deep, sophisticated gray. You buy a new white Ikea drawer set for extra storage because you saw it on a YouTube dream desk tour. You buy a new bluetooth speaker and the airPods for noise-cancelling to help you get into a flow state. Okay, I admit I'm not perfect you guys!

As previously mentioned, ways to avoid the Diderot effect are: establishing a money roadblock, calculating your spending in hours worked, utilizing the 30/30 rule, and asking yourself if you could afford 5. Find a system that works for you to avoid buying new things to match your new things.

Source: James Clear "The Diderot Effect: Why We Want Things We Don't Need — And What to Do About It"

Reminder: Get **10 bonus hacks** and more at
www.TheMoneyResolution.com/HackIt

PART 4

Money Minimalism

CHAPTER THIRTEEN

Take On A Money Minimalist Mindset

There are a few misconceptions when it comes to taking on a minimalist lifestyle. Many think it means giving everything away, living with nothing, and having barely enough to get by. Some think it means living out of a suitcase and wearing a plain black tee day after day. Others look towards the creepy, empty interiors of Kim Kardashian's mansion and shudder. In actuality, it's quite different than any of these assumptions.

Minimalism is living with less and being decisive with all of your purchases, belongings, and happiness. Sure, that might start with one dramatic cleanse of unnecessary belongings, but it leads to beautiful realizations about our obsession to consume. We are wired to addiction. Advertising and the media reinforce it. FOMO and access to buy anything at the touch of a finger reinforce it. Often, even the people we spend the most time with reinforce it. But what if you could learn to say no? What if you could learn to let go? What if you could conquer your desire for more? What if you could learn to simplify?

Okay, let's bring this back to the topic at hand. How can one apply the principles of minimalism to their finances? It's actually a perfect through line you'll see. Once you're comfortable with the idea of detaching your happiness from buying, using, and collecting things, you'll start to find that this new outlook can positively impact your net worth. The minimalist doesn't focus on everything. The minimalist doesn't get distracted. They focus on simplifying, what matters, and a long-term plan.

As a bonus, you might find like I did that applying minimalist principles to your life and money can have the added benefit of improving your productivity. In the end, I'll share my minimalist approach to writing this very chapter!

71. MIS EN PLACE (YOUR MONEY)

Mis en place is a French culinary term meaning "everything in its place." Take this approach and apply it to your money and financial resources.

One of the best things about removing clutter and simplifying your life and finances is that you know where everything is. You know how to find what you need so you can quickly access it when you need it.

There are a few specific ways to apply this to your personal finances. For me, it's organizing all of my logins in a browser folder, spending 5 minutes a day working on my money, and, most importantly, telling my money what to do and where to go via automation. I don't let money I need to save stay in my bank account for more than half a day. I've set up where these funds should automatically move to, aligned to my payday schedule. The same is true when it comes to paying off my credit cards in full each month.

I don't obsess over my credit score because alerts will tell me if it changes. I don't lose sleep thinking about passwords and hackers because I've chosen credit cards and banks that have security protections. The point is, get organized, pay yourself first automatically, and do your research to find the best tools and resources for your needs. After that, you can, for the most part, set it and forget it.

"Everything in its place" relates to more than this. Find a budget or tracker you like. Try out new FinTech that helps you see all of your accounts in one literal place. Or take a DIY approach by hand if that's your thing. Find your system and tools and keep it simple. This is the most effective way to plan, prep, and be ready for everything life can, and inevitably will, throw at you.

72. LEARN TO SAY NO

"…what do I feel is the next right move for me?"
-Oprah

A 2018 Credit Karma study, which polled over 1,000 U.S. consumers, found that 39% of millennials have spent money they didn't have and gone into debt to keep up with their peers. And not shockingly, nearly three-quarters have kept this money issue a secret. Further, over 27% of millennials polled admitted to "feeling uncomfortable saying no" to friends suggesting activities they can't afford and 36% of respondents admitted they think they will go into debt within the next year if they continue keeping up with friends. This has become a major issue for millennials; their inability to say no to having a good time, even when they know they cannot afford the concert, weekend trip, sporting event, or international vacation.

Okay, you get it. The data shows saying yes and and giving in to FOMO is putting us out. Oftentimes, we can't even fully enjoy the thing we're doing while it's happening because of the dread of the bill. Case in point, the last time you were at a restaurant and everyone agreed to order another round *plus* dessert.

So how do you avoid that? How do you actually say no? It's actually pretty easy. You simply say, "Sorry I can't. I have plans." Or even just, "Sorry I can't." While difficult to do at first, it becomes easier over time and you might be surprised how people react to it. Don't make an excuse. Don't feel bad. Don't lie. Plans for you doesn't have to mean a prior social arrangement or another significant commitment. You can make plans to stay in. To read a book. To work on a hobby. To update your budget and goals. To cook an awesome meal. To call your mom. To watch The Notebook for the tenth time. It really doesn't matter because here's the thing: they likely won't ask. Think about it. Would you?

Hopefully you're already saying no to things you don't want to do. The trick is to learn to say no to the things you *do* want to do, but know you can't afford.

73. UTILIZE THE 80/20 RULE

"80% of the results come from 20% of the causes.
A few things are important; most are not."
-Richard Koch

The 80/20 Rule, also known as the Pareto Principle, suggests that 20% of your activities will account for 80% of your results. In the simplest terms, it's identifying the actions that are most productive and prioritizing those. It's prioritizing what is most effective, to ultimately achieve even better results.

One misconception with this rule is that some falsely interpret it to mean you should focus solely on the top 20% and ignore taking action on the other 80% of the work. Let's think about studying for an exam. It would be wise to start with the chapters and concepts you think will most likely be included. However, if you stopped there, you risk failing altogether. Start with, and spend the most time with, the concepts most likely to appear on the exam. From there, you might consider moving onto the concepts that trip you up the most. After that, study everything else chronologically. Your odds of success improve dramatically when you create a plan and attack the challenge with intentionality.

You can apply this rule to almost any situation, including your own finances. By doing so, you can organize your thoughts and hone in on the essentials first and let go of everything else. In Chapter 1, I provided ways to create lists to help you prioritize your to-dos when it comes to your finances. Today, This Week, Someday aligns perfectly with this 80/20 rule! The 100% Decision does as well. Both of these are great exercises in simplifying and prioritizing.

You can't pay off debt, save, improve your credit, pursue financial education, invest, and retire all at once. But you can start with a goal and list out the most impactful steps to get you to that goal. If you want to start investing, you might first want to prioritize paying off your credit card debt. If you want to eliminate your debt, you might decide to focus on paying off your high-interest cards first. You should NOT prioritize taking online surveys to earn $1 an hour or cutting coupons to save at the grocery store. Focus on what is most important and give yourself permission to let go of everything else.

You could even apply the 80/20 rule to this book and internalizing money hacks to suit your needs. Realistically, as much as I tried to include the most relevant and useful content, I recognize that for some of you, only half, a third, or even 20% makes sense to prioritize and take action on. That's totally okay! In fact, I consider it a win if you start applying 20% of this book to your life. My hope is that you get the most out of this book with the least amount of wasted time.

Source: Investopedia "The 80/20 Rule"

74. CREATE YOUR 25/5 LIST

This step combines the two previous steps into one great exercise I hope you'll consider participating in. This 3-step strategy was made famous by Warren Buffett after a conversation he had with his private pilot (I know). They went through this exercise after Buffett expressed disappointment that his pilot was still working for him after so many years. Here's how it works...

Step 1. Write down 25 goals or things you'd like to do or accomplish (as it relates to your money). These can be a mix of short term and long term action items. I encourage you to stop right now and *actually* do this. This exercise is MOST effective if you stop what you're doing right now and participate without reading further...

Not done? Then why are you looking down here? Participate!
I'll even say "please."
I'm just filling up spaces and lines.
You know, so you don't look ahead...
Done?

GREAT!

Nice job.

That was a close one...

Step 2. Circle five, and only five, of the most important goals. This part is a challenge because by now you love your goals and might feel attached to all of them. I hear you. Even if this feels like picking your favorite child, do so now. Then read on...

When Warren Buffett asked his pilot what he was going to do with the other 20 items, he was disappointed to hear his pilot say he would work on them intermittently as he tackled his top 5. "No. You've got it wrong. Everything you didn't circle just became your Avoid-At-All-Cost list. No matter what, these things get no attention from you until you've succeeded with your top 5."

Step 3. Focus on your top 5 goals and say no to the rest. To be sure this is extra clear, at this point, anything that is NOT circled you must avoid-at-all-cost until your top 5 are complete. Only then can you move beyond. Another tip is to start the same exercise over with a fresh list of 25 items.

Ultimately, the objective is to simplify your goal setting process and help you spend time on what matters most. Now you know why it's important to say no. You understand the value of the 80/20 rule. Now you have a concrete action plan to help you tackle your top 5 (yes, that's 20% of 25) money tasks without distraction.

Go Beyond: Applying the 25/5 rule to your finances is a great thing to do, but don't stop there. You can apply the 25/5 strategy to everyday life and other goals. For example, if you're looking to get fit or lose weight, what are the 5 changes you can focus on to get there? If you want to grow your business and have a million ideas, write out your list and focus on your top 5 ideas. If you're the average of the 5 people you spend the most time with, try to spend more time with the 5 people you most respect and admire. Apparently, good things come in fives! Like virtual high-fives.

75. BECOME A CLOSET MINIMALIST

In many cases, closets are the most cluttered spaces in our houses. Partly because, as consumers, we're trained to believe there are 52 seasons in a year... It doesn't take long for us to grow tired of our wardrobe and struggle to piece together an outfit in the morning. There's a constant urge to buy more but clothes are expensive, even at trendy thrift stores. So, here are 3 concrete, spend-free ways to help you avoid frivolous splurges on clothes.

Makeover What You Have.
One of the only things I enjoy about Facebook is reading through comments when people ask for suggestions. One I came upon recently led to a brilliant idea I implemented. The question was about finding the best way to start fresh with a wardrobe. One commenter said, "Whenever I feel tired of my clothes and am tempted to buy more, I give my closet a makeover instead. I give things away I don't wear. I iron and dry clean items that need attention. I stain remove and repair buttons. And voila, what was old and tired is new again. I always find things I had forgotten about and love!" Brilliant.

The Hanger Hack.
One way to find out what you don't wear is to try this hanger trick: turn all of your hanging items one way. For example, the hook of the hanger comes from the back of the closet to the front. When you wear it and put it back, flip the hanger the other way. After a month or two you'll have a clear visual of your favorites and the pieces you can live without and give away.

Remember, No One Cares.
When you're having that moment of panic when you're getting ready for work or a date, remind yourself: nobody notices or cares or will remember. Your clothes are a lot like that zit you woke up with on

your nose in high school. You thought EVERYBODY was judging you. But I assure you, everyone was thinking about their own zit, or outfit, or new hairstyle that day. The point is to refresh, pare down, keep it simple, and remember the old adage that I'm probably making up: "an outfit does not a person make."

Spend a few hours this weekend and spruce up your closet. Try out the hanger trick. Learn to underthink your outfit each day. Your clothes are uniquely you. If you got it, rock it. But not those holey socks. Ditch those!

76. MEDITATE

Yep. I said meditate. And that's a money hack. Stay with me on this one...

In an interview with CNBC, Grant Sabatier, author of "Financial Freedom", recommended taking five minutes every morning to take part in a "money meditation." In this time, you can expose yourself to the source of your money anxiety and work towards overcoming it one day at a time. By grounding yourself each morning around your finances, you can get comfortable with volatility in the market and learn to leave emotions behind. Plus, to connect this to an earlier hack, he specifically called out 5 minutes!

In my very non-professional opinion, there are many ways to meditate. Some meditation styles center around clearing your mind, while others want you to let your thoughts wander wherever they please. You might want to consider the Calm app or practice Yoga. You will need to experiment with a few of these ideas to find what works for you and see if any of them can help you with personal finance. Meditation, or deep critical self-reflection, can help you unlock your feelings about money. It can also help you unlock your goals and even your path to achievement.

If you think you've never meditated and feel hesitant to try, you might be wrong. Have you ever taken a hot shower and let your mind wander? You likely come out with deep epiphanies and life-changing inspiration, like *What if Santa Claus is real, and our parents just give us gifts to hide the fact that we're on the naughty list?* (r/Showerthoughts). For me, deep reflection on a singular topic is sitting on my deck with a cold brew in the morning or a cold beer in the evening, headphones on, with books and my notebook nearby just in case. This is my meditation. It often starts with writing or reading Kiplinger and then bam. For 30 seconds I go down a mental rabbit hole. An idea sparks. Creative thinking takes over. I zone out. I relax as worries melt away. I noticeably feel about 10% happier than when I sat down.

Find what works for you or double down on your mindfulness habits. That might occur while driving to work, while walking during a lunch break, or even in the middle of the night when you can't sleep. Everyone has moments of deep reflection. Recognize these moments and catalogue what you think most about. Recognize your fantasies and goals. And then, write them down… and dig into them. Unpack them a bit more. Don't suppress your thoughts and desires. Acknowledge them and then take action. The point is, you need to look within before you can fully understand your Why. Looking within will help you unlock how much is *enough*. It might help you identify what you should focus on next.

Pro Tip: Journaling can be its own form of meditation that might have similar benefits. Many of us have notebooks that help us stay organized for work or school. You might use digital planners to keep track of your day. But a personal journal is an underrated resource. I challenge you to start a personal productivity journal. This is the perfect place to keep track of that "Ta-Da" list or document your "Today, This Week, Someday" list. A productivity journal is a perfect place for budgeting or goal-setting. You can also try bullet journaling. There are lots of YouTube tutorials so I won't walk through the details here but it's a simple, clean, very organized way of planning your time and helping you unlock the essentials. Purchase an affordable physical notebook or open up a doc on your computer, and put reflective thoughts to words!

---

77. DITCH THE BUDGET

I, a self-professed finance nerd, do not budget. Budgets are no fun. The best way to turn you, the reader, off is to tell you to budget and how. Even if you are motivated to start a budget today, you're likely to abandon it in a few months, weeks, or even days. Why? Because budgets are boring, no fun, finger-wagging, guilt-inducing, jump-scare nightmares. Good in theory, bad in practice. Budgets are like diets: exciting to think about, painful in practice.

If you want to lose weight, you change your eating, sleeping, and exercise habits. If you want to do better with your money, you change your spending and saving habits. Can a budget help get you there? Potentially to start. But only if it helps you build habits that stick, like utilizing automation to remove emotion from the equation. Instead, what I recommend if you're just getting started is tracking your spending by category. Your past behavior is the biggest indication of future spending and it will help you identify categorical spending you can improve. For me, this is a once-a-year sit down exercise at the very beginning of the year. If you want to do this on an ongoing basis, I recommend free services like Personal Capital or Mint.

My bank account at any given moment might make you cringe. My "savings" sits at $500. My Checking fluctuates but is almost always below $500. Why? Because I know exactly where my money is coming from and exactly where it is going. For the most part, I don't have to pay attention to it all because it's on autopilot. I tell my money where to go and what to do when it hits my account. My savings (in a high-interest online savings account), retirement funds, and credit cards automatically draw money from my paycheck or checking account each month so I never have to make the choice to spend or save.

Why do I do this? So I'm not tempted to spend it. Seeing my low balance when I check my account is a daily reminder that "money is tight." It's tight because I choose for it to be. I push myself to save 50% of everything I earn. I Pay. Myself. First. Via. Automation. It's routine and it's extremely satisfying. Plus, it saves me time and mental stress.

Chris Reining, self-made millionaire who was featured on CNBC's Make It, explained this well when he said, "I automated my money years ago and the benefit is, I don't have to make decisions about where my money should go, how much I should invest, what I can spend, do I have enough savings and so on."

What about budgeting for upcoming expenses like a wedding or travel? In that case, you might want to budget and back into your goals. Then automate. One fun way I saved for travel was to gamify it. I "tipped myself" $5 every time I went to the gym. Double instant gratification. Guilt-free money to spend on my next trip AND a total fit beach body? Win-win.

78. TECH CLEANSE

Find the source of your FOMO (Instagram). Track your usage via your phone (or Instagram). Consider removing your biggest time sucks (Instagram) or creating a barrier (deleting the Instagram app). Don't let tech (Instagram) bully you into debt.

I document almost everything in life via photos on my phone, like many of us. But I never feel compelled to instantly share or add to "my story" ten times a day. Because even the act of doing so means opening my phone and going on social sites where I see an amalgamation of people's best style, travel, and consumerism highlights and I'm bombarded by ads that can genuinely freak me out. I know posting isn't just posting. It's the anxiety of overthinking filters, hoping people like it, and going down dangerous rabbit holes. I almost never feel better after scrolling through social feeds.

I'm not going to tell you exactly how to do this. I just want to challenge your thinking, your relationship with technology. What adds value and what detracts from your happiness? I encourage you to take action. Unfollow distant friends and exes. Find other ways to organize and share your photos. I love making photo books via Shutterfly, making scrapbooks filled with memories, and albums with polaroid pictures. You know, like people used to do. In terms of buying, shop for tech based on durability and functionality, not features and brand names. Use your tech until you can't. Buy used. Leave the house without your phone. And when you get home, do the unthinkable...

call someone you're thinking about to say hello and catch up. Try a day without using your devices on the weekend. You can do it. You might find that less tech can be more.

...says the guy who just wrote this entire chapter on his phone using voice dictation. *That* was my minimalist hack to writing this chapter! And you know what, it worked! I finished it faster than usual and I enjoyed feeling like speaking directly to you, the reader. Plus, it forced me to slow down and be deliberate. Another reminder that hacking life, finances, productivity, and more is all about experimentation and trying something new.

I should go post a quote about that on Facebook... insert winking emoji!

Pro Tip: Surround yourself with good people AND good apps? As many have said before, you are the average of the 5 people you spend the most time with. Taken further: I'd argue you are the sum of the 5 apps/websites you use the most. Garbage in, garbage out. Don't take this too literally but take some time to reflect on this. Are you opening Facebook, Instagram, Amazon, and Netflix the most daily? Or are you opening Kindle, Coursera, Reddit, Google News, and YouTube (for the right reasons) the most? I'm not here to judge or try to tell you scientifically this is black and white, good and bad. I'm here to ask you to think critically about the time you spend on your devices. What percentage of that time is helping you learn? Helping you move closer to your goals? Helping you broaden your thinking? Helping you help nurture and grow your financial intelligence (FQ)?

***

CHAPTER FOURTEEN
Invest Like A Minimalist

"You don't have to be rich to invest.
But you have to invest to be rich."
-Bradley J. Sugars

I almost titled this chapter: Investing: A Deeper Dive (But Still The Shallow End Where You Belong)...

I used to work in the jewelry industry. One day my boss said to me, "For most people, buying a diamond is the thing we spend the most money on that we know the least about." True, I thought to myself. Several years later I realized he was wrong. *Investing* is the thing we spend the most money on that we know the least about. The good news? You can still be a great investor with a little knowledge and a LOT of keeping it simple. If less is more, simpler is better. Especially when it comes to your investments. As the saying goes, don't let perfect be the enemy of good.

I'll admit it. I'm an egregious over-thinker. I'm already overthinking if the word egregious is the perfect adjective there... and as much as I love to travel, sometimes I spend more time researching and creating daily agendas than I spend being on vacation. Yes, I'm that guy...

I've learned that when it comes to personal finance and investing, analysis paralysis is a real thing. But if there's one take-away I hope you internalize from this book, it is this: stop thinking and just start. Too basic of a hack? That's the point. Seriously, put this book down right now and do something, anything!

As someone who obsesses over education in personal finance, I find there is far too much theory and critical analysis. You don't need a retirement savings compound interest rule of 72 chart to get moving. You don't have to research individual stocks or meet with a financial adviser "when you find the time." Get a Vanguard mutual fund that tracks the S&P 500 or total stock market. I use TD Ameritrade. You can use Vanguard directly or Fidelity. Just pick and go.

Do I up my 401(k) or start a Roth IRA? Should I invest in a mutual fund OR an ETF? And isn't a recession coming?! The answer to all of that is yes, and it doesn't matter. Do both. Do it all with small amounts to start.

I promise you this: you can learn as time goes on, but you can't earn if you're not invested. You don't score on the sidelines. You already knew all this. But sometimes we just need to hear it... Money does grow on (metaphorical) trees. But you *must* plant the seeds for it to grow, gradually then suddenly. So, let's get planting.

79. DOLLAR-COST AVERAGE INTO THE MARKET

For many of us, the best method when it comes to investing is the *ostrich strategy*. What's that, you ask? It's all about burying your head in the sand to avoid something (e.g. investing) altogether. I get it. The world of investing seems vast and complicated. I just called it a "world" for goodness' sake!

To help simplify, there's a saying I love and abide by when it comes to investing: "slow is smooth, smooth is fast." Those who react quickly without thought will make mistakes. I can thank the Navy SEALs for that adage.

That's where the dollar-cost averaging strategy comes into play. Here's how it works: when you dollar-cost average into the market, you invest the same amount of money at set intervals no matter what. The best way to do this is via automation (for me it's every payday). The reason? It's time IN the market (not timing the market) that matters most. The best time to invest was 20 years ago. The second best time is *today*.

If this sounds complicated, I assure you dollar-cost averaging is meant to do the exact opposite—make investing decisions easy and automated. By the way, if you have a 401(k) you're likely already doing this! By the way, if you do have a 401(k), you're already an experienced investor. Isn't that cool? You've been buying into the market on a steady and consistent basis and technically have a "diversified portfolio". See, it's not so scary if you keep it simple and consistent. Do not panic, do not hurry. A dropping market is not a threat, it's an **opportunity** to invest our capital at higher yields and to rebalance our portfolios. By keeping calm and being deliberate in our decisions, we can turn panic into growing income. By remaining calm when the market is panicking around us, we can identify value. And there is value in slow and steady growth.

Ignore the news and this week's trend. Case in point: the coronavirus pandemic has led to investing panic and has caused the market to drop 33% in the last week as I write this. My reaction? Do nothing differently. Stay the course. And stop reading the daily headlines. Sometimes it pays off to keep your head in the sand after all…

As financial expert and author JL Collins puts it, "When it comes to investing, once you have the basics down, the less you pay attention, the better off you will be."

Read Next: Seeking Alpha "Turning Panic Into Income"

80. INVEST IN THE TOTAL STOCK MARKET

I recently went to the horse races for the first time and learned a lesson very quickly: always bet on the favored horse, not the horse that has never won before. You can apply this thinking to investing. The biggest indicator of a stock's future performance is its past performance. Therefore, when picking your investments, you should always bet on the favored horse. The problem? You still might lose. The only way to know you'll bet on the winning horse every time is to bet on ALL the horses. Don't pick individual stocks. Pick a basket of stocks. This is the simplest and best approach for beginners.

As previously mentioned, analysis paralysis is a real thing. That is why I encourage you to pick a total stock market index fund and invest in it regularly. If this fund is a mutual fund, you can set up automatic investments, something you cannot do with an exchange-traded fund (ETF). This starting point is well-diversified and can be cheap in terms of fees to get started. Plus, an index can't crash to zero like individual stocks can. Not to mention, index funds beat 85% of all actively managed mutual funds after fees.

To keep your strategy simple, my recommendation is to have roughly 70-80% of your funds invested in a total stock market index fund. The rest should be in low-risk bonds. This ratio should shift away from the total stock market and lean into bonds the closer you get to retirement.

Okay, but there are several options. You might be wondering which one you should pick? My suggestion is the Vanguard Total Stock Market Index Fund (VTSAX, Mutual Fund) or the Vanguard Total Stock Market (VTI, Exchange-Traded Fund) to, again, minimize fees and maximize growth.

Whatever you do, remember this: not investing is one of the riskiest things you can do with your money. Even with your cash sitting on the sidelines in a high-interest online savings account, it will struggle to keep up with inflation year after year. So put that idle cash to work and buy *all* the stocks at once. Stick to the basics, then stay the course. Because an object in motion is likely to stay in motion.

81. INVEST IN THIS ORDER

"Become an owner, not a consumer.
That'll change your life."
-Tony Robbins

First off, according to a recent Gallup study, 45% of Americans do not own any stocks, which includes individual stocks as well as stocks included in mutual funds or retirement savings accounts like a 401(k) or IRA. If you're on the other side of this study, that's great! You're already ahead of many. Now, let's make sure you're buying into the market and saving towards retirement in an optimized manner because there are lots of accounts and tax implications to get your head around. As with many things money, there is no one-size-fits-all plan, but this suggestion is a simplified starting point to follow.

To get this out of the way first, the last place I recommend buying stocks is in a personal brokerage account. In fact, for emphasis, I'm not even including it in the list below because I recommend you max out all of your tax-advantaged accounts before you even consider picking your own funds or stocks with your post-tax money. You should *always* start with tax-advantaged accounts:

401(k) or 403(b):

Invest in your company-sponsored retirement account with pre-tax dollars. If your company offers any sort of match, always contribute up to that amount at a minimum. After reaching the match, you may want to consider the Roth IRA and HSA below before coming back to your 401(k) and contributing more. The annual 401(k) contribution limit as of 2020 is $19,500. As difficult as it might sound, I encourage you to try contributing to the max as a goal. If you don't qualify for a 401(k), consider a Traditional IRA (instead of a Roth IRA) to earn a tax deduction for your contribution and to grow your investments tax-deferred, meaning you'll pay income taxes when you withdraw invested money. The drawback is that the maximum contribution is roughly a third of the 401(k) option.

Roth IRA:

Next up is one of my favorite accounts. The great thing about a Roth IRA is that money going into a Roth IRA has already been taxed. Therefore, your investments grow tax-free (as opposed to tax-deferred) and you will not owe taxes on distributions from this account come retirement. The annual contribution limit as of 2020 is $6,000 and once again, I suggest you aim to hit this maximum each year. If you also contribute to a Traditional IRA, that also counts towards the $6,000 annual maximum.

HSA:

This is my actual favorite account. I always recommend the Health Savings Account (HSA) option over a Flexible Spending Account, if you have both available to you. This is because HSAs offer triple tax benefits. Money goes in before tax, money grows tax-free, and you can spend the money tax-free on eligible medical expenses in retirement. The annual contribution limit as of 2020 is $3,550. You must self-direct your HSA investments so be sure to invest the amount of money you're allowed to annually. Generally, you can invest any HSA funds in the account over $1,000 or $2,000.

If you're able to max out all 3 of these tax benefit accounts, you would have set aside $29,050 this year towards retirement, nearly all of it invested. Only then would I recommend you look at other accounts such as a 529 to save towards education or a SEP IRA if you earn income on the side, or a personal brokerage account.

Source: The College Investor "The Best Order of Operations for Saving for Retirement"

82. GET THE MOST OUT OF YOUR 401(K)

One of the great things about saving into a 401(k) account is the simplicity of setting it up and delegating what portion of your paycheck you'd like to set aside every payday automatically. However, this is where most people stop and there are several steps you can take over time to ensure you're getting the most out of your 401(k) or similar accounts like a 403(b).

Increase your contribution later in your career.

At age 50, your annual contribution limit dramatically rises as a way to help those who are behind in retirement savings catch up, so to speak. This additional catch-up limit for savers over 50 was increased to

$6,500 in 2020. Therefore, as of 2020, people over 50 can contribute up to $26,000 towards their 401(k): $19,500 annual limit plus $6,500 catch-up contribution. If your employer allows after-tax contributions (or if you're self-employed) you can save even more. If you're not behind, I still recommend you take advantage of these extra savings while in your higher-earning years.

Manage your investment risk.
As we learned in 2020 due to COVID-19, a large drop in the market can devastate your retirement savings. An aggressive investment plan early in your career is encouraged because your portfolio has time to fully recover and then some. However, as you enter the middle of your working career, and especially the final years of your working career, you'll want to ensure your 401(k) investments offer proper diversification with broad exposure across a variety of asset classes. A simple target-date fund could do the trick, since these become less risky as you approach the intended retirement year (which can be found in the name of the fund itself).

Re-check your plan annually.
First and foremost, you want to make sure that you are avoiding funds with high fees by looking to see if other funds now offer better rates. High fees eat into your investment gains and may cause you to increase your contributions or even delay your retirement. It's also good to check if new asset classes might have been added that are challenging to find in the real world. Since 401(k)s offer lower prices than you'd find with an individual brokerage account, these new funds might be worth looking into further. Most plans only offer around 25 options, so doing a little research annually into these funds won't require a herculean effort.

Take your 401(k) with you.
Today, on average, it is common for people to change jobs every 3-4 years. Unfortunately, far too many people cash out their 401(k)s, facing stiff penalties and taxes, or leave them behind and uninvested. Instead, I recommend you roll 401(k)s from your previous jobs into your new

work plan's retirement account or, at the very least, your traditional IRA if your current company's plan does not permit this transfer.

Never borrow against your 401(k).
That's about all there is to it. It might be tempting to dip into that money to treat yourself to something, but it's not worth it. Let that money grow and compound, you'll thank yourself later.

Pro Tip: Give yourself a 401(k) raise. Ideally, you'll make the maximum allowable contribution each year to an employer-sponsored fund, such as a 401(k). Again, for 2020, that's $19,500. As you move up the career ladder, put raises into your retirement savings instead of spending them. As previously mentioned, this is the perfect place to bank 100% of a windfall, such as a bonus, as well.

Sources: Investopedia "Strategies to Maximize your 401(k)" & Kiplinger "Already Contributing to Your 401(k)? Here's How to Optimize It..."

83. TRADE WITHOUT COMMISSION FEES

DIY investing has never been easier. Now there are tools and tech available to us to help us invest on our own as we've never had before. Even better than trading with ease? Trading for free!

2019 was the YEAR of no-fee trading. By the end of 2019, most major online brokers eliminated commissions for standard online-initiated stock trades. Likely inspired by (and to keep up with) Robinhood's no-fee trading structure, many of the biggest brokerages decided to cut their trade commission fees completely, and it all happened in a matter of weeks in October after Charles Schwab made their no fee announcement. Gone are the days of TV ads boasting $4.99 flat-fee trading or commissions commonly costing $6.95. A new era of investing has begun as it seems the race to the bottom has ended... in a tie at $0!

Great. You can now buy index funds that do not require high management fees or any trading fees. But why is this so powerful and important? While $5 doesn't sound like a lot, especially if you're trading with $1,000 or more, over time this $5 could have grown exponentially instead of eating away at your compounding returns. Let's run through an example provided by The Ascent, A Motley Fool Company:

Let's say you set aside $1,000 annually to invest across 5 individual stocks. At a $6.95 fee per trade, you're now effectively investing just $965. Based on a 10% rate of return, over 20 years that portfolio would have earned an extra $2,000 without fees. Over 30 years, it would have earned nearly $5,800 extra. With no-fee trading, that $5,800 goes back into your metaphorical pocket.

It's not a stretch to say that "zero is the new normal" when it comes to stock trading commissions. This is a win for investors, especially for beginner investors with limited funds available, who could save hundreds or even thousands in trading fees alone. While I'm not an advocate of picking stocks via a personal brokerage account, you can now do so if you choose to with no fees, making it slightly more palatable if you have excess cash sitting idle. The one downside (and a word of caution) is the temptation to overtrade. Instead, stay focused on the long-term and enjoy even more compounding benefits because of commission-free stock trading.

What changes could be next? In early 2020, Robinhood added the option to purchase fractional shares. Schwab followed suit. It seems likely this will become a common feature among all the major brokerages in the future. This is especially helpful if you wanted to buy stock in high-valued companies like Amazon, which was approaching $2,000 a share at the start of 2020.

84. CONTRIBUTE TO LAST YEAR'S IRA

As previously covered, each year from January 1st through December 31st you're able to contribute towards your Traditional and/or Roth IRA up to the combined limit of $6,000 in 2020. However, what many don't realize is that December 31st technically isn't your last chance to contribute up to the max. You actually have until you file your taxes the *following year* to contribute to the previous year's IRAs.

It's extremely simple to do so. In almost all cases between December 31 and up until tax day, when you make a contribution to your IRA account, you should now see an option to toggle between putting the money towards the last year or the current year. Always contribute to last year's IRA first. If the contribution is to your Traditional IRA, this will even reduce your taxable income for the prior year, which will come in handy when you do file your taxes. If you're wondering if you can open a Traditional or Roth IRA after January 1st and still contribute to the previous year if you haven't filed your taxes, the answer is yes—you can!

Why do this? Perhaps you weren't able to reach the max and you received a holiday or new year bonus or have a new, higher-paying job. Perhaps you've worked through the math and figured out you may owe the IRS money so you'd rather reduce your tax bill by contributing to a Traditional IRA. Regardless, contribute to last year's IRA first if you're eligible to do so before contributing to the current year so you have the ability to put the maximum contribution towards both years.

Two final reminders: do not contribute over the maximum or you will face a penalty tax, and there is an income limit when it comes to the Roth IRA (there is none with a Traditional IRA). As of 2020, you are only eligible to open one if you made under $139,000 in the previous year.

Source: Money Under 30 "Making Prior Year IRA Contributions"

CHAPTER FIFTEEN
Play With F.I.R.E.

"FI is not about running away from the things you hate in life. It's about running toward something."
-Choose FI: Your Blueprint To Financial Independence (book)

By far, my favorite trending hashtag of 2019 was #MillennialRetirementPlans. Here are a few examples from Twitter:

- #MillennialRetirementPlans A van down by the river (@starlightinflight)
- #MillennialRetirementPlans Hope the parents prepared for my retirement too (@accountdiane)
- #MillennialRetirementPlans Selling old participation trophies as nostalgia (@brnekked42)
- #MillennialRetirementPlans Why is this even on trending? We all know we'll never be able to retire. (@rachelg1919)

And my personal favorite:

- #MillennialRetirementPlans Work yourself to death and you won't have to worry about retirement (@jenninjuice1)

As you can see, most millennials don't feel prepared to retire "on time", so the thought of *early* retirement must feel like a total joke. The reality is, it isn't as far fetched as it seems. That's where F.I.R.E. comes in.

First off, what is F.I.R.E.? It stands for "Financial Independence, Retire Early." It is a relatively new, inspiring movement in personal finance. We are talking about extreme frugality and extreme savers set on escaping the 9 to 5 and retiring before the age of 40. They march towards this goal by saving 60%, 70%, and even 80% of their income in the pursuit of financial independence and early retirement. What does the average American save towards retirement? Try five percent.

According to The Penny Hoarder, "Financial independence means you're at a place where you can live solely off your investments—but it can also mean you have enough money coming in from passive sources, real estate, and even freelance and part-time passion projects to pay the bills (and then some)."

Personally, I'm inspired by this movement but haven't gone as far as saving three-quarters of my income. However, following F.I.R.E. principles, I have been able to save half of my income and this has helped me picture a far different life than most of my peers. My #MillennialRetirementPlans have come into focus and I have the F.I.R.E. movement and hard work to thank. While I won't be retiring before 40, F.I.R.E. has allowed me to set a goal to retire before 50. In fact, 45 is my stretch goal.

While the F.I.R.E. lifestyle isn't completely for me, I learned a lot immersing myself in the movement that has helped me reassess my values and goals. After all, retiring early is the ultimate life hack and the math is shockingly simple. Just ask "Mr. Money Mustache" himself.

85. KNOW YOUR FI NUMBER: THE 4% RULE

Here's how to calculate your FI (Financial Independence) number, which is the total amount of money you would need to have invested so that the amount generated from the interest on your assets can sustain you, without you having to work in order to earn an income again.

To calculate your FI number, determine your total estimated annual expenses during retirement (be sure to consider inflation of 2% annually). Next, multiple your projected annual expenses by 25. This formula is often called the "multiply by 25 rule".

For example, if your projected annual expenses are $40,000, you'll need $1,000,000 to retire and live off of 4% of your portfolio annually. By leaving the remaining 96% of your nest egg invested, that money will continue to grow annually at an assumed earnings rate minimum of 5%, enough to sustain you until the end of your life (assuming future stock performance is consistent with historical performance). This gives you a very concrete idea of where you need to get to and allows you to decide when you hope to get there by determining how much you want to save to reach your goals.

From here it's up to you in terms of how to get there. Cut mercilessly on the things you don't love. Side hustle. Create a passive income stream or two. Continue your financial literacy journey. Invest consistently. Surround yourself with good people. And incorporate daily money hacks from this book and lessons from my first book "The Money Resolution". Simple, right? Of course not. But it's enjoying the journey that matters most. Don't forget, that's the best part.

This is a super simplified breakdown of an incredibly popular topic. This isn't so much a tactical hack as much as it is a high-level overview of the ultimate life hacks. There are dozens of books committed to the F.I.R.E. movement. For more, I recommend "Playing With FIRE" and "Passive Income, Aggressive Retirement." I also recommend the subreddit r/financialindependence and my favorite YouTube channel on the topic: "Our Rich Journey."

Read on: Good Morning America "This couple retired early using the FIRE method. Here are their top tips."

86. ADHERE TO THESE F.I.R.E. PRINCIPLES

Abiding by F.I.R.E. principles does not mean you are officially thereby here within elected as an official ambassador to the F.I.R.E. movement community crew and organization (sarcasm extremely intended). It's not a cult but I understand why the unaccustomed make assumptions in that regard. However, there are massive lessons to be learned, tremendous savings to be had, and incredible habits to be developed if you choose to accept a few key components of the philosophy:

- Develop a can-do mindset. Believe it to achieve it. Avoid limiting beliefs and acceptance of the status quo.
- Start as soon as possible. Save early and often so that you can take full advantage of compound interest.
- Save until it hurts. Get comfortable with being financially uncomfortable day-to-day. Personally, I get *uncomfortable* when my checking account hits 4-figures. I'd much rather tell my money what to do and automate my way to that.
- Calculate how much retirement income you need to cover all basic living expenses first. Then move onto potential wants.
- Diversify. The key is to not lose money but you might (see also: will) take a hit day-to-day or week-to-week. But diversification and dividends will ease the blow during rocky waters and staying the course means you'll eventually find smooth sailing.
- Control what you can control. Your current tax rate is part of that.

It's worth noting, several previously-covered hacks overlap with F.I.R.E. principles such as banking 100% of your windfalls, the 30/30 shopping rule, going two-wheeling, and house hacking.

Additionally, F.I.R.E. seekers adopt a lifetime learner mentality and invest in themselves. F.I.R.E. seekers read daily and listen to podcasts that educate, not just entertain. They double down on what they are strong at, develop emerging skills or interests, and focus on what matters most as it pertains to their wealth and personal happiness.

87. PAY FEWER TAXES

You can save hundreds of thousands of dollars in taxes in your lifetime. Do I have your attention? F.I.R.E. seekers are nodding in unison right now...

For many, taxes in the United States feel completely unfair and overly complicated to understand. I get it. If I'm being honest, it took me a long time to get my head around tax brackets and I'd rather do just about anything else than work on filing my taxes. At least, that's how I used to feel...

In time I learned that if you understand a few tax basics, you can reduce your taxable income with just a few easy moves throughout the year, allowing you to hang onto much more of your hard earned income. Here are a few of those tips and hacks you may want to consider to help you gain a leg up when it comes to paying Uncle Sam.

- Defer as much as possible in your 401(k) and Traditional IRA because it lowers your income tax liability, *today*.
- Set up a Roth Conversion Ladder. The basic idea is to take money from tax-deferred retirement accounts, pay income tax on this money now, then convert the funds to a Roth account where you'll never have to pay taxes on it again. This is especially useful if you're a low-income earner now. By doing this, your money can grow tax-free!
- Harvest capital losses and gains in taxable accounts. Some "robo-advisors" like Betterment and Wealthfront do this for you automatically.
- You can contribute to a 457(b) account AND other work-sponsored accounts in the same year. Money can be withdrawn before age 59.5 without penalty.
- While a little more complicated, a backdoor Roth IRA is an option to consider if you are over the income limit for eligibility for Roth IRA contributions ($139,000 in 2020). There's even a MEGA Backdoor Roth IRA option if you're feeling extra.
- Consider a Roth 401(k) instead if this option is available to you. Similar to a traditional 401(k), this is also a tax benefit retirement account. The key difference, however, is that employee contributions are made with after tax money. In short: pay taxes now, pay none on qualified distributions later in retirement. You should consider this if you think you'll be

in a higher tax-bracket in retirement since withdrawals are tax free.

- Self-employed? There are various tax-advantaged accounts available to you. My favorite? The SEP IRA if you're a small business owner with no or few employees. You can contribute $57,000 in 2020 or 25% of net self-employed earning (whichever is lesser). Distributions in retirement are taxed as income and there is no Roth version of this account.

Feel inspired? Great. Keep going with your learning and research! I recommend Chapter 6 of the "Choose FI" book for starters, the Bigger Pockets Money Podcast, and The Stacking Benjamin's course called "Learn How To (legally) Cheat On Your Taxes." Perhaps (legal) cheaters DO prosper!

88. DRAWDOWN YOUR RETIREMENT ACCOUNTS IN THIS ORDER

In retirement, it's important you have a plan for tapping into your savings if you want long-term financial security. For starters, focus on maximizing returns on your capital investments. In simple terms, if you take invested money out first, you're eliminating the opportunity for that money to continue to grow. This is crucial because you may be in retirement for 30 years or more. Therefore, the faster those assets generate more gains, the slower you'll draw down your retirement funds. In other words, taking out too much too early hurts your current nest egg *and* future earning opportunity.

There is no simple set it and forget it approach. However, the order of withdrawals is where efficiency is maximized. With that in mind, the following is a super simplified suggestion and not the end-all-be-all-definite-list of what you should do IRL. This is a starting place to help illustrate key points.

First off, once you reach age 59 ½ (as of 2020 in the United States) you can access any of your retirement accounts without penalty. Early on in retirement, you're likely going to be in a relatively low tax bracket because, for the most part, your income is only what you're taking out of your accounts. You will owe taxes on these funds so withdraw only what you need to live off of. Specifically, start with any 401(k) or 403(b) funds you have.

Another reason for this is to reduce the number of Required Minimum Distributions (RMDs) you need to take out, which start April 1st the year after you turn 72. As a reminder, at age 72 you are required to take annual distributions from your 401(k). If left alone, this money would grow and your distribution would be much higher, in turn triggering more taxes. The penalty for failing to withdraw the correct amount is a stiff 50% of the amount that should have been withdrawn. Ouch!

Next up, it is optimal to begin tapping into personal investments and your Health Savings Account (HSA) if you have one. Ideally, your HSA is invested and growing. Using this account on eligible medical expenses means you won't owe any taxes on the money you spend.

Finally, upon reaching age 70 ½, you should begin tapping into your Roth IRA and Roth 401(k) if you haven't already to minimize the tax burden of RMDs since Roth IRAs do not require minimum distributions. This invested money is growing tax-free so either you or your beneficiary can take out and use this money without owing taxes on it as regular earned income.

Regardless of your withdrawal approach, I recommend you take out money on a consistent monthly or quarterly basis rather than all at once at the beginning of the year, so that you can allow cash you're not ready to use now to stay invested and grow. Set reminders or, even better, set up automation with each account to avoid forgetting.

When it comes to pensions and social security, these are added benefits but not something I recommend you calculate into your future projections. These would be a bonus, but not something to bank on. A cherry on top if you will.

Despite complications and challenges, it is possible to create a drawdown strategy to best optimize both your tax burden and your investment growth. Many advisory firms use software to help you determine the best method and order to dip into funds to create a personalized strategy.

To say this section is just scratching the surface would be an understatement. It is incredibly important to continue your research as you approach retirement or work with a professional advisor to create your optimal plan, because your drawdown plan should also be consistently monitored and tweaked. Knowing the rules is a great starting point, but a DIY approach is only recommended for those willing to dig into the details of each account.

Source: Seeking Alpha "Order Of Withdrawals For Your Retirement Assets"

89. ACHIEVE A FI ALTERNATIVE

Achieving F.I.R.E. means that you could reasonably live off of your investments and other assets for the rest of your life regardless of whether or not you continue to work. But it's the "retire early" part of the acronym that rubs some people the wrong way.

David Bach, author of "The Latte Factor", prefers to call it F.I.T.E.: financial independence, transition early. Paula Pant, writer and podcast host of "Afford Anything" preaches several mini-retirements to pursue a passion called "retiring early and often". But for the purpose of explaining alternative paths, let's focus solely on different ways of achieving financial independence. Whether the individual or couple decides to formally retire from all work or not after achieving FI is up to them. Freedom of choice is the goal. Here are four alternatives to explore that differ slightly from traditional F.I.R.E. principles:

Lean FI
In retirement, individuals seeking Lean FI plan to live off an income of less than $40,000 a year, and oftentimes considerably less than that. The advantage is the amount of time it takes to get to FI is much shorter than other strategies. Save aggressively now, live off less later as well. The pro is that work becomes optional much sooner.

Fat FI

This allows you to live off an upper-middle-class income come retirement. This number will vary depending on location, but a common number is an annual income of $100,000. This means you'd need to have no less than $2.5 million invested based on the 4% growth rate to be financially independent. With Fat FI, it will take you longer to reach financial independence but allows you to live off of a pretty healthy income in retirement.

Slow FI

Slow financial independence aims to strike a balance between enjoying the process as much as the destination. This may be as simple as maxing out a 401(k) each year but little else in terms of saving or investing.

Coast FI

For younger folks, spend the next couple of years savings as aggressively as you can. Then you pull the foot off the gas pedal for the rest of your working career while your early investments grow and have a better opportunity to compound.

90. SET A MONEY RESOLUTION

This F.I.R.E. stuff can sound pretty intimidating and overwhelming if this is the first time you're hearing about it. Retire in 10 years? That sounds extreme to most people. But here's what's not extreme to get you on the path: set a one-year money resolution.

I obviously recommend my first book, "The Money Resolution: 101 Ways To Save Money, Make, Money & Get Out Of Debt In One Year" as the perfect place to start. It contains all the foundational steps I took to get out of credit card debt, improve my credit score, lower my bills, travel on the cheap, learn to invest and lots more! Like this book, it also comes with a 101 step checklist organized in the back. In it I challenged readers to try to tackle 80 steps in one year if they are truly getting started on getting good with money from scratch.

There are lots of other ways to change the direction of your life and, at the very least, shave a couple of years off of your working life. There's no single-path blueprint for changing your financial life. It takes goals, hard work, sacrifice, and a commitment to learning continuously. You don't know what you don't know, so an ongoing learning plan is a necessity for radical improvement.

It's important to remember, January 1 is not your only chance to set a resolution. A resolution is a 365-day commitment. It's a dedication to change and make improvements in your life. And when it comes to your money, a good place to start could be as simple as eliminating one bad habit or creating a new good habit over the upcoming year that will stick.

PART 5

Hacking Financial Education

CHAPTER SIXTEEN

Financial Education Hacks

"It was literally easier for me to become the youngest woman in American history elected to Congress than it is to pay off my student loan debt."
-Alexandria Ocasio-Cortez

Preach A.O.C.! According to the Washington Post, education expenses have climbed 65% in the past decade. According to a SoFi commercial I saw while watching the World Series, 44 million Americans are in student loan debt. According to the YouTube channel Two Cents, "1 in 5 millennials expects to die without ever getting out of debt." One. In. Five. Clearly, to say this is a problem would be an understatement.

I'm no exception. But I only keep my student loans around to help me feel young. Kidding. But that is the exact kind of crazy thought that DOES happen when you walk in student loan debt shoes year after year…

Not to mention we got into this debt mess because they never taught us about financial education in ANY of the 13 grades (if you count kindergarten) we attended and sorry I'll get off my soapbox but WHY?! We have a LOT to talk about. I'm starting to use all caps so let's get back to hacking…

91. START A 529 PLAN

There's no denying that college (for yourself or for your children) is a big-ticket expense. And like all big-ticket expenses it's best to be prepared by saving a little over a long period of time rather than playing emergency catch-up when your kids become high schoolers. That's where 529 plans come into play.

A 529 plan, called such because it is authorized by Section 529 of the federal tax code (I'm sure you weren't wondering...), is a tax-advantaged savings plan intended to be used for college education, tuition at an elementary or secondary school, or other education-related expenses.

How do you find the right 529 plan for you? I recommend you compare plans at savingforcollege.com. The good people there help you learn about college savings; open, connect and monitor a 529 plan; and even accelerate your savings growth. Even if you don't have a child now, but plan to in the near-ish future, you should start searching for a plan that works for you.

In my state of Washington, the website let me know that Washington is one of 16 states that does not offer residents a state income tax benefit for 529 plan contributions, "so shop around." Then it provided me with two plan options in my state and a long list of other plan options including Vanguard and TD Ameritrade. Filters and ratings can help you drill down into what's most important to help you find the right plan for you.

A few other noteworthy callouts regarding 529 plans via savingforcollege.com:

- In addition to federal tax savings, 34 states currently offer a full or partial tax deduction or credit for 529 plan contributions.
- Like a Roth IRA, the owner of the account is allowed to take out any funds that they put in at any time for any reason without penalty. Just be sure to leave the earnings alone so you don't face a penalty, unless you are withdrawing for a qualified reason.
- Most plans allow you to take a "set it and forget it" approach by linking directly to your bank account to automate your investments.

- There are no restrictions to get started. You can contribute any investment amount on any income at any age, regardless of who the beneficiary is.

It's never too early to be thinking about education and a 529 plan offers a tax perk that helps nudge you go from thinking about college to saving towards it. With that said, I would not prioritize this over saving for your own retirement and definitely don't prioritize this over paying off high-interest debt like credit cards or your own student loans. Help yourself before helping others, especially because there are opportunities to earn financial aid in the form of grants, low interest loans, and scholarships as a starting point. But, if you're in a good financial position to do so, opening a 529 plan could be an excellent option!

> **Pro Tip:** Some employers allow payroll deduction into 529 plans. This is a great, relatively-new perk that some places of work are offering. Unfortunately, "some" means just 11%, according to the Society for Human Resource Management. Of those "some", a handful even offer a contribution match, similar to a 401(k) plan. While this doesn't offer any kind of tax benefit, it does allow you to set money aside towards education automatically before it ever hits your bank account because automation is everything!

92. TRY ONE OR MORE OF THESE STUDENT LOAN DEBT PAYOFF HACKS

According to Tina Hay, author and CEO of "Napkin Finance", "At more than $1.5 trillion, if Americans' student loans were a country, they would be the thirteenth largest economy in the world—roughly the size of Australia." Yes, this is a real problem, but you already knew that… If you're like me, you understand *shoulda, woulda, coulda* doesn't help now. Rather than give you tips and suggestions for avoiding student loan debt in the first place, I'm going to approach this as a realist and speak directly to those of you dealing with a small mountain of student loan debt (listen up: self).

- Use the "avalanche" approach to tackle your loans with the highest interest rate first. This, of course, makes the most mathematical sense.
- Begin paying before your interest begins. In many cases, there's a "grace period" where you aren't required to make payments. Instead, start paying as soon as possible before interest begins the grave digging process. Too morbid?
- Make payments biweekly as opposed to monthly. Like the mortgage payment hack, by changing your payment schedule you will end up paying 13 months worth of dues in just one year.
- Consider loan consolidation and refinancing. This tip is especially important if you took out private loans to pay for college. If not, you may lose benefits that come along with federal student loans.
- Put this thought out of mind: "One day my loans will be forgiven." I have never personally met anyone that has successfully gotten their loans forgiven. Rather, this thought process reinforces the *kick the can down the road* mentality. That's an uphill road by the way...
- Pay more than the minimum. Not a hack. Just plain simple and smart. It works for your credit card, it works for your student loans.
- Sign up for auto debit if your lender offers a discount. These commonly range from 0.25% to 0.50%.
- Use your interest tax write off money in full to make an additional payment towards your loans. This deduction allows you to earn $2,500 in interest as an above the line exclusion. Talk about paying it directly forward!

These 8 tips are great. But there's one more that may be available to you that I wanted to bring to your attention...

93. PAY OFF YOUR STUDENT LOAN DEBT THROUGH WORK

I love bennies, benjamins, and... peanut butter?

While not yet common, some employers have programs that allow employees to set aside money from their paychecks to go directly towards their outstanding student loans. Further, companies can even make contributions towards employees' student loan balances.

Peanut Butter is a benefits administration firm that provides student loan assistance. If you're wondering, it's named after the condiment that was a key staple in the college diet... Working directly with companies like Peanut Butter, employers can set up student loan repayment options for employees. Firms like Peanut Butter eliminate the need for added staff to manage and maintain the program. In addition, Peanut Butter claims to provide insights, advice, counseling, and refinancing options. It's not just a perk, it's an educational resource.

According to a study by Peanut Butter*, programs like this are shown to improve company retention by 36%, reduce turnover costs, attract new talent, and even build a more diverse workforce. A 2017 study by Oliver Wyman surveyed over 3,000 households with a bachelor's degree or more and found nearly half felt student loan repayment was the most preferred perk or benefit, more important than 401(k) contributions and health insurance. Yes, it's *that* important, especially to millennials in the workforce.

The cost to employers? A flat annual fee and an additional administrative fee for each employee that receives your contribution. For a medium-sized business of roughly 300, this shakes out to just $2,500 a year for company-wide access and $5 per repayment plan participant. If this sounds like a sales pitch, it's not. I just think it is a *really* cool program and I would LOVE to work for a company that provides such an opportunity!

*Study conducted by Peanut Butter in July, 2015 via focus group interviews and email surveys to 400 qualified respondents ages 20 to 35 years old with at least "some college" education.

> **Pro Tip:** More and more employers are offering financial wellness programs, including debt management programs, budgeting advice, and education about the basics of the financial markets. If that's a free resource available to you, be sure to take advantage. Better yet, be an advocate for such a program if this is not currently offered at your work!

94. SKIP COLLEGE

Wut? I know. I can't believe I just said that either! But put away the pitchforks and hear me out...

Let's start with the most obvious argument for choosing not to attend college: the spiraling cost of higher education. According to The Atlantic, "The price of consumer goods has increased by a factor of four since the late 1970s. College costs have increased by a factor of 14." Student loan debt has become a major financial burden, a common reason why many millennials delay major life milestones like buying a house, getting married, and having a family. In fact, as of February 2018, the average college graduate had an average of $37,000 in student loan debt. 1% had over $100,000 in debt.

Plus, here's a commonly known reality: most college graduates end up in jobs that did not align with their majors and many end up in jobs that do not require college degrees in the first place. According to the Department of Labor, 1 in 3 college graduates had a job that required a high school diploma or less in 2012. We're talking bartenders, taxi drivers, and janitors.

And finally, and this is the big one, many people succeed without a college degree. Extreme examples include: Richard Branson, Ellen Degeneres, Walt Disney, Bill Gates, Steve Jobs, and Mark Zuckerberg. Okay, odds are your kiddo isn't the next Mark Zuckerberg. But, you might be surprised to learn about some of the highest paying jobs you can earn without a degree. So instead, the real hack here is to consider a certificate program, an excellent alternative to a degree program. The best paying job opportunities that these certificate programs lead to include: Web Developer, Construction and Building Inspector,

Industrial Engineering Technician, Pipefitter and Plumber, Court Reporter, Sheet Metal Worker, and more.

Even without a degree, and sometimes without a certificate, here are the top 10 best paying jobs with median salaries and projected job growth rate through 2026 (according to the U.S. Bureau of Labor Statistics as of July 2019):

10. First-line Supervisors of Fire Fighting & Prevention Workers: $76,330 (+7.2%)

9. Power Plant Operator: $79,610 (+1.3%)

8. Elevator Installer & Repairer: $79,780 (+12.1%)

7. Electrical & Electronics Repairers: $80,200 (+3.7%)

6. Detective & Criminal Investigator: $81,920 (+4.5%)

5. Commercial Pilot: $82,240 (+3.8%)

4. Power Distributors & Dispatchers: $86,410 (-2.5%)

3. First-line Supervisors of the Police: $89,030 (+6.6%)

2. Nuclear Power Plant Operator: $94,350 (-10.2%)

1. Transportation, Storage and Distribution Managers: $94,730 (+6.7%)

To land one of these jobs you more than likely need a high school diploma. You also might have to earn a certificate or license, spend a certain number of years training on the job, and/or possibly to pass a test or two. However, the point is, none of these require a college degree and all of them have a median average salary over $75,000.

Not to mention, you can learn just about anything online! Online courses are all the rage these days. I'm working on one myself! Check out www.themoneyresolution.com/course to learn more. For free education, I always recommend YouTube. I especially recommend subscribing to The Money Resolution once there. But I digress...

CHAPTER SEVENTEEN

Become a Lifetime Learner

"An investment in knowledge pays the best interest"
-Benjamin Franklin

I truly believe personal finance is the missing link in the American education system. Luckily, we've started to make some progress. 19 states now require financial literacy in their public schools with bills in Rhode Island and North Carolina pending. Even so, not all of those mandates are created equally. Only 6 states require it as a stand alone class. The rest require it as a part of another class such as math or economics.

Requiring financial education in schools makes so much sense when you think about it. Research has shown that requiring high school students to take a personal finance course reduces their likelihood of taking out expensive payday loans down the road. Not to mention, financial literacy can literally be the difference between life and death for some, as health care systems become more and more expensive and difficult to navigate.

Unfortunately, for most millennials, gen Xers and baby boomers, schools taught us how to be an employee, not how to become wealthy. Because of this, roughly 70% of Americans are financially illiterate. Among U.S. adults, just 34% can get at least 4 questions right on a basic 5-question financial literacy quiz, according to the FINRA Investor Education Foundation (you better believe I'm quizzing you at the end of this chapter!).

So what makes ongoing education a hack? Education is a lot like compound interest. In fact, I call it compound knowledge. When you commit yourself to learning about personal finance and applying best practices, you quickly understand that knowledge and action are bigger than the sum of their parts. You find that growing your wealth happens gradually, then suddenly.

Education can change your life, no matter your situation and starting point. Building a solid educational foundation can go a long way when it comes to understanding and managing your finances. Continuing to build on that foundation delivers exponential returns. Teachers are an excellent resource in school. But who can you learn from IRL outside of school? I'm glad (I pretended) you asked!

95. FIND A PERSONAL FINANCE MENTOR

According to Wells Fargo, finance is the most difficult topic to discuss with others. 44% of their survey respondents selected finance ahead of religion (32%), politics (35%), and even death (38%). Yes, even death. What's the best way to tackle your biggest anxieties? Talk to someone! Anyone! Well, maybe not anyone. Nobody should have to listen to Uncle Jerry's speculative investment of the month at the family barbecue... hard pass, Jerry!

When most people think of talking to someone about their financial situation, their mind instantly conjures up a financial planner. Sure, that's smart and we'll talk about that next but, I actually want to recommend finding a "money mentor" first. Why? For many reasons, but my favorite is that it might not cost you a dime outside of your time and attention!

There are actually lots of options when it comes to finding a mentor but I recommend you start within your circle. Think of people in your family or friend group that have similar goals or have experienced successes that align with the financial life you seek to live. This could be someone that recently bought a house, has an awesome side-hustle, or "lives for free" by house hacking. It could also be someone that lives a similar lifestyle to the one you want to live—

think: has a family, travels often, owns a business or retired early. This person might even be a sibling, best friend, or parent. If so, that's great! Make the most of that close treasure trove of information!

If you have somebody in mind you know a little less well, you may want to ask a few basic questions first to make sure your values align and that they don't have any ulterior motives. Tell them what you admire about them, then ask questions like: *Did you have a money or business mentor? How do you go about making financial decisions that involve risk? What are your future goals as it relates to earning money or even spending it?*

Before having that conversation, it's good to ask yourself some questions as well. *What are your goals? What is your biggest hurdle or fear? What are you most interested in learning that this person specifically can help you learn?* Know what you're hoping to get out of the relationship before you begin. This will also help your mentor know the best way to tailor their knowledge to your goals and keep conversations focused.

Once you find your mentor, I recommend setting time aside monthly to meet up and chat. I think you'll quickly find there's something truly powerful about saying your goals out loud to somebody else, especially somebody you admire that will hold you accountable. From there, be sure to listen closely, literally take notes, and constantly take action based on your mentor's suggestions.

Best of luck finding your money mentor or partner in finance. Whether you're saving for a dream vacation, looking to pay off your student loans, or stashing away money for the purchase of your first home, a mentor can play a critical role in helping you achieve your goals. Don't forget to say thank you and pay it forward when you're in a position to do so!

96. MEET WITH A FINANCIAL PLANNER

Mentors are great for offering big-picture advice and sharing their own stories, but a financial planner can help you create a full financial plan customized exclusively for you and your unique situation. Asking a mentor for help is an excellent place to start. Paying a financial planner for help is how you can fill in gaps and create an action plan.

Okay, I get it. Meeting with a financial planner might sound worse than seeing the dentist twice a year. First, it's not as scary as it sounds, and second, expanding your knowledge is probably more useful than having plaque scraped off your teeth! Well, it's more interesting at least...

Financial planners obviously don't work for free. They're professionals after all. A financial planner's fee will, in almost all cases, pay for itself over time if you use their excellent advice. Look at it as a necessary checkup or preventative maintenance. If nothing else, it will force you to take the time to sit down and take a long, hard critical look at your financial situation, your goals, and your future.

How do you find the right financial planner for you? And how do you know that they are giving you information that you can trust? Let's tackle the trust factor first.

Financial planners have a legal duty to act in your best interest—as opposed to pushing you towards an investment fund for the sake of earning commission or benefitting in any other way. This is called fiduciary duty. They are legally and ethically bound to give you advice that is best for you. Not all financial planners are required to put you first. But, you can avoid the bad ones by making sure you find a *fiduciary* financial planner, because it doesn't get better than "legally bound."

Finding one is a slightly more complicated answer, but still relatively easy. First off, you'll want to know your budget, what services you need, and if you want to meet in-person or online. Meeting virtually is one way to save costs. One resource I recommend is the search tool by the National Association of Personal Finance Advisors (NAPFA.org). It takes just seconds to find nearby fiduciary financial planners that are legally bound to act in your best interest. In addition, GarrettPlanningNetwork.com also offers a map of the U.S. where you can click on your state to find a listing of financial planners who cater more to the middle class.

Now you know how to find a financial planner you can trust. But what does it look like to meet with one? You won't be sitting down to pick individual stocks to bet red or black on. More than anything, it's behavior coaching, not asset selection. Look at it as having a financial therapist. Sure, you will strategize and take action and maybe even purchase funds, but they will help fill in educational gaps and encourage questions. They are fully aware that you didn't ditch out on Personal Finance 101; it was never taught to you in the first place!

Great, but how much does it cost? You can control this too! Many people think financial planners are only for the rich, but the cost for their services can vary widely. Your cost will usually depend on your portfolio (how many assets you currently need managed) and your arrangement. For example, if you're okay with a DIY approach, you can set up a fee-only planning arrangement. This means meeting with a financial planner does not have to equal a long-term relationship with constant meetings. In fact, this might just be a one-time meeting. Once the plan is set, it's now simply up to you to follow it. But, of course, it's always useful to get that plan updated as you reach certain life milestones, for an additional fee. The choice is yours!

Pro Tip: If you simply can't get over your mentor or financial planner-phobia, talk to normal, everyday human beings. Money has become such a taboo topic but it doesn't have to be! We're all earning it, spending it, and stressed about it. So why do we go through all of that on our own or, at best, with our significant other? Here's the takeaway: if we don't talk openly about money, we won't learn and get better with it.

---

97. USE THESE RESOURCES

"The more you learn, the more you earn."
-Warren Buffett

There's a reason I call myself a "self-proclaimed personal finance nerd." I consume media on all things personal finance every spare moment I have. I don't yet dream in numbers and charts but I'm sure that's coming soon! Sometimes we all just need some good ol' fashioned personal recommendations so here are some from a certified money nerd to help you find your next page-turner or podcast go-to.

Note: I also gave a list of recommendations in "The Money Resolution" so this list avoids repeats and only consists of resources I have devoured since publishing that book.

Books

- Happy Money by Ken Honda
- Choose FI: Your Blueprint To Financial Independence by Chris Mamula, Brad Barrett, and Jonathan Mendonsa
- Napkin Finance by Tina Hay
- Passive Income, Aggressive Retirement by Rachel Richards
- Quit Like A Millionaire by Kristy Shen and Bryce Leung
- The One Thing by Gary Keller
- Company of One by Paul Jarvis
- Kiplinger's Personal Finance (Magazine)

Websites

- Reddit.com/r/PersonalFinance
- Reddit.com/r/FinancialIndependence
- MoneyUnder30.com
- MoneyCrashers.com
- BiggerPockets.com/blog
- TheSkimm.com/Money
- Girlboss.com/Money
- Facebook.com/TheMoneyResolution

YouTube

- Graham Stephan
- Two Cents
- Andrei Jikh
- Meet Kevin

- Our Rich Journey
- Jeff Rose
- Ask Sebby
- Nate O'Brien
- Investing with Rose

Podcasts

- Choose FI
- Your Money's Worth
- This Is Uncomfortable
- Smart Money by NerdWallet
- Bigger Pockets Money
- Financial Grownup
- The Money Nerds Podcast
- Money With Friends
- Entrepreneurs On Fire
- Frugal Friends
- Side Hustle School
- The John Chapman Show

Movies & Shows

- Playing With FIRE
- Becoming Warren Buffett
- Crackle's Going From Broke

98. TEST YOUR KNOWLEDGE

If you're here and you've read this book in order, you're either feeling slightly overwhelmed (I hope not) or well educated and motivated (I hope so!). Regardless, let's put this knowledge to the test! Try this quiz created by AIG Retirement Services. Hint: answers are in the back of the book at the end of the Conclusion... but do try this on your own first!

1. If a late payment is sent to a collections agency, how long will it remain on your credit history even if you have paid it off?

    A) Less than a year

    B) 1 to 3 years

    C) 4 to 5 years

    D) 6 to 7 years

2. What is the formula for calculating your net worth?

    A) Assets plus liabilities

    B) Liabilities minus assets

    C) Assets minus liabilities

    D) Assets divided by liabilities

3. Imagine that the interest rate on your savings account was 1% per year and inflation was 2% per year. After one year would your ability to buy something with the money in this account be:

    A) More than today

    B) Exactly the same

    C) Less than today

4. Which of the following about federal student loans is not true?

    A) For certain federal-loan programs, the interest on your loans is paid for by the federal government while you are in school and during grace periods

    B) Your parents must sign a promissory note before loan funds are distributed

    C) Entrance loan counseling for all first-time borrowers is required

    D) You will have to pay back your student loans even if you do not complete your degree or find employment after college

5. If you have too many credit cards, what should you most consider doing?

    A) Close as many as possible

    B) Request a higher credit limit

    C) Be cautious about closing cards

D) Close cards with the lowest balances

6. As a general rule, how many months' expenses do financial planners recommend that you set aside in an emergency fund?
    A) 1 to 3 months' expenses
    B) 3 to 6 months' expenses
    C) 6 to 12 months' expenses
    D) 12 to 15 months' expenses

If you struggled with this quiz, fear not. You're not alone! The study by AIG and EVERFI tested 25,000 students and 20% got just 1 question right. More than half got just 2 or fewer right. If you got 3 or more right, you're in the minority so great job! Plus, "general rules" aren't fair for testing (looking at you #6) but point proven nonetheless. This quiz illustrates that financial education is still elusive for most of us. As a country, we clearly have a long way to go.

Education is the best investment you can make. Many of the rich understood this long ago. We can get angry at the rising cost of tuition. We can question the value of a college degree. We can blame the missing gap in our education system. But we can't debate that becoming a lifelong learner of personal finance is the best way you can continue to grow your wealth, and it's never too late to learn.

Education is the most valuable asset you will ever own, an asset that can't be wiped out by a bear market. Financial literacy helps you survive a personal financial emergency. It helps you stay the course, even in the midst of a pandemic. It can help you grow your wealth gradually, then suddenly. The best part? It's transferable if you take the time to pay it forward. The worst part? It can erode...

That's why it's so important to continue education as a lifetime learner in one form or another. This could be training or taking a personal development course. This might mean going back to school or adding a certificate to help you in a work-related field. It could be as simple as watching YouTube videos or taking an online course. I'm obviously a huge advocate of reading books!

Speaking of, you've come a long way in reading this one! The final chapter contains just a few hacks that are more philosophical than educational but I would argue they are just as important as anything you can learn from a classroom, a mentor, a financial planner, or online quiz.

Listen to Next: Money With Friends Podcast "The simple, six-question personal finance quiz that more than 50 percent of college students failed"

CHAPTER EIGHTEEN

Money Mantras & Financial Superpowers

"Live your life like you're the hero in your own movie."
-Joe Rogan

Try and learn. Experiment and fail. Succeed and replicate. That's the essence of hacking. No matter the outcome, you are helping yourself by taking action and prioritizing money. By now you've learned it's important to be a student of money forever, especially because we weren't taught money in school or, in many cases, at home.

When I began my money resolution at the beginning of 2018, I came across many rules of thumb and money mantras like "pay yourself first". Another in particular stood out to me early on because it was less easy to grasp: "pay it forward". I didn't think much of it at first. In fact, I thought to myself: *How can I help others when I have nothing to my name?*

However, as I learned about money via constant consumption of knowledge, took action via small efforts day in and day out, and ultimately changed my financial trajectory for good, I started to reconsider my ability to "pay it forward." The day I became net worth positive for the first time in... well... ever, it became crystal clear. I wrote and published *"The Money Resolution"* in less than 2 months in an effort to share everything I learned with anyone that would listen. I knew my tips worked for me and that I could help provide a proven and actionable path that could help others as well.

By now, it's likely you understand the language of money. But there are two words that aren't often mentioned in financial literacy that I want to emphasize in this final chapter. Those words are *gratitude* and *giving*. Here's why these two words are so important in your financial journey and how they help you hone and level up your financial superpowers...

99. EXPRESS GRATITUDE & MAKE YOUR MONEY SMILE

Many of us blame money for our problems and think that more money will solve them. Yet, as we earn more, the cycle doesn't stop. We quickly fall into the trap of needing more. Instead, it's incredibly important that we constantly reflect on how fortunate we are and find happiness in exactly what we have.

In his book "Happy Money", author Ken Honda begins by asking if your money is smiling. He emphasizes why it is so important to say thank you when you receive money as well as when you spend or give your money. Your money can smile no matter the amount you earn or have if you learn to appreciate it. When you appreciate, things appreciate. He explains that he learned this lesson from his money mentor 30 years ago.

How exactly can you express gratitude and make your money happy in your daily life? Here are a few examples:

Keep a gratitude journal
Set aside time daily or weekly to write down what you're grateful for. Some recommend doing this first thing in the morning, but regardless of the time it helps to be very specific.

Write a letter of gratitude
Not an email. Not a Facebook chat. Write a letter and send it through the mail. Tell a family member, friend, or mentor why you appreciate them. This has shown to increase your own happiness and it will certainly make that person's day.

Repeat positive affirmations out loud

Create your list and read it out loud anytime you feel negative or hit a roadblock. For example, "I am wealthy in more ways than one. I choose to live a rich and full life. I have the power to build wealth. Every dollar I spend or give comes back to me multiplied."

Use visual cues as reminders

This could be a simple sticky note on your bathroom mirror or computer monitor. It might be a framed quote on your desk. The idea is to trigger daily thoughts of gratitude. In sight, in mind!

Use positive language

Focus on things in your control and speak about what you have, not what you lack. Naturally, you might notice yourself smiling more, saying thank you more often, and finding yourself around other positive people.

Author Melanie Badey might have summed it up best when she wrote, "Gratitude unlocks the fullness of life. It turns what we have into enough, and more. It turns denial into acceptance, chaos to order, confusion to clarity. It can turn a meal into a feast, a house into a home, a stranger into a friend. Gratitude makes sense of our past, brings peace for today and creates a vision for tomorrow."

Your past doesn't define you. You are in control of your mentality each day going forward and you become what you believe. If you express gratitude and positivity when it comes to your money, you (and your money) will smile more.

100. GIVE

> "From what we get, we can make a living;
> what we give, however, makes a life."
> -Arthur Ashe

When was the last time you gave? How did it make you feel?

If you don't remember... I want you to think about why you

haven't recently. In almost all cases, the answer we tell ourselves is that we would give more if we made or had more. But here's the reality: generosity isn't likely to change when you make more because it's a fundamental mindset. If you don't give when you make just a little bit of money, odds are you still won't give when you make more. This is the reason I encourage everybody, no matter your income, debts, or situation, to give. Giving becomes a habit.

Many people don't give because of the scarcity mindset. They believe they will only earn a finite amount of money and they will absolutely need it all. However, the wealth you will receive in your life is not finite. You can always earn more and grow your wealth, especially with ongoing education and action. There is no need to hold on to your money so tightly when having it gives you the power to help others and the freedom to receive it in return if you ever find yourself in need.

Making more money doesn't change your heart. It just reveals more of the same. Being generous is a choice we make. It's like choosing to be happy and grateful, instead of negative and angry. If you feel inspired but genuinely don't have the means to give, there are many other ways to build this habit. You can give time. You can give thanks. You can give emotional support. You can give knowledge. You can give things you own to charity or a Goodwill. When you're done with this book you can give it to a friend. And of course, you can give love.

The best part about giving? It's contagious. And it's damn good for the soul.

But, of course, this is an action-driven book. Here are three specific ways you can give today and in the future that you may not have thought about:

Determine how much you can give each month and automate it.
This helps you factor charitable donations into your monthly budget. At the very least, automatically move money into a "give-only" saving account each paycheck. Remember, any amount is great, especially if you're just getting started. For example, every $1 donated to Feeding America can translate to a distribution of 10 meals!

Use Charity Navigator to help you find a cause or organization.
Charity Navigator is the nation's largest and most-utilized evaluator of charities. They assess over 9,000 of America's best-known and some lesser-known, but worthy charities.

Put your giftable money in a donor-advised fund (DAF).
DAFs let you donate without choosing a specific charity right away. The best part is your money can grow tax free until it is gifted. According to Consumer Reports, these funds are the fastest form of philanthropy today and make up 12% of individual giving.

If you get stuck choosing a cause, organization or DAF, you can always give to the arts, your local newspaper, and education. One of my favorite things to do is browse and support Kickstarter projects for example. There is no single right way to give because all giving is great!

101. USE & HONE YOUR UNIQUE FINANCIAL SUPERPOWERS

If movies and comic books have taught us anything, it's that superheroes come in all forms. The same can be said when it comes to your superpowers. By now, you probably have a good sense of your strengths, weaknesses, and opportunities. The key is to recognize your skills and principles (plural!) and continuously develop them to level up your finances and grow your wealth. Utilize your strengths and values in a way that is most optimal for your unique situation.

Here are examples of financial superpowers you might recognize from within (I encourage you to highlight ones that resonate with you!):

You are a numbers person.
You understand how to budget and recognize the power of compound interest and the importance of starting early.

You are able to take a long-term view.
Retirement is not a mountain to climb but a staircase with steps to guide you on your journey.

You are a compassionate, generous person.
The well-being of others is constantly at the forefront of your mind. Your daily mission is to help others.

You know how to define success on your own terms.
You understand the harm in comparing. The only person you compare yourself to is future you.

You are a social leader and educator.
You have the ability to teach others what you learn and get excited about collaboration towards common goals.

You are an underdog.
You have faced many challenges and know you are not meant to succeed in life, especially financially. This is why you will.

You are a humble, naturally frugal person.
You have always understood the importance of living within your means and making your money go further.

You are an entrepreneur.
You have a business mindset. You come up with ideas to solve other people's problems and want to work for yourself.

You are a creative thinker.
You see challenges as opportunities to think differently. You are willing to try new things and approaches. You are open to learning and okay with failure.

Reflect on and write down who you are. You might find you are a hybrid of the above personality traits. It might be something completely different. Identify your unique strengths and skills. Hone them. Use them to hack money and have fun.

No matter your unique skills or superpowers, *always remember to help yourself first, then help others. Say thank you. Be grateful. Give. And repeat. You'll soon find yourself, and your money, smiling.*

Conclusion: How Much Is Enough?

"The people who are crazy enough to think that they can change the world, are the ones who do."
-Steve Jobs

Try this. Reread the Steve Jobs quote above but this time replace "the world" with "their life."

It's about time YOU think differently. Don't accept the status quo. Change things. Push forward. You don't have to be a genius. You just have to believe that you can change *your* world. You can change *your* life. Not to be rich, but to live rich. Look within and make the decision to replace negative thinking with positive thoughts. Accept your flaws, your past, and your current situation. Know that you won't be perfect with every step and every decision. You will make mistakes but you will not disappoint yourself if you make the choice to commit, trust yourself, and enjoy the journey.

Success is a mindset. Like giving, positivity is contagious. Your mentality becomes your reality. Success begets more success and it can snowball quickly. What you appreciate, appreciates. In the finance world we would call this "compound returns."

But there is one more lesson I hope to impart as we part, and it's actually more of a question I hope you'll reflect on: How much is *enough*?

Ask yourself this as you set your goals. Ask yourself this as you search for a mentor, discover momentum, and ultimately enjoy success. Resolve to get good with money and commit to action, but also reflect on what it is you truly need and *why*. It's easy to become obsessed with earning, saving, and paying down debt, but it's equally easy to lose sight of what truly matters or fall back into bad habits. Many people get just as good at spending as they do at earning. They think the answer is more. And the cycle continues...

"It is not the man who has too little,
but the man who craves more, that is poor."
-Seneca

Studies have shown that lottery winners tend to return to their original level of happiness once the novelty has worn off. On the opposite end of the spectrum, the same has shown to be true for those that lose their legs. It's devastating at first, but after rehabilitation, people tend to return back to their original level of happiness. This is known as the *hedonic treadmill* and it works on a small scale too. For example, the first bite of dessert is much more satisfying than the 3rd, 5th, or 10th. The point is, you are in control of your own happiness and no amount of money is going to solve that. Because, as the saying goes, everywhere you go, there you are. Control what you can control, enjoy everything else along the way.

I learned this lesson at a young age. When I was ten years old, I played The Sims for the first time on our family computer. After struggling to get a job, a virtual wife, and *enough* money, I decided to take to the interwebs to see if I could find a cheat code to help me get ahead and expand my house. I really *needed* to buy that ridiculous bearskin rug, paint the walls a new color, and add a second floor. Fifteen minutes later, I discovered gold: an infinite money cheat code.

You better believe I had a blast on my shopping and building spree... for about thirty minutes. You see, I quickly realized I was no longer having fun. But why is that? I had it all! Yet, I was missing something valuable: appreciation. I wasn't earning this success during this simulation. I rushed to get to the end and missed the entire point of the game. I wasn't grateful for what I had because I didn't earn it. All my wanting became exhausting and I gave in to my desire for more. In all of that, I forgot about how much fun the journey is.

I'm not saying earning more and adding on to the house of your dreams is a bad thing. I am saying to enjoy the process and slow down. Live with intentionality. Spend with intentionality. Believe in yourself, but don't be in a hurry.

I fear you may have seen the title of this book and thought I was selling a cheat code. The reality is there is no such thing. However, I hope I inspired a new way of thinking. I hope I helped you tap into your creative brain. I hope you know how to prioritize money as a tool —a tool that can help you get to where you want to go. I hope you feel armed with know-how and confidence. I hope you're excited to enjoy the ride! But most importantly, I hope you feel guided by your *why*, know your *enough*, and are ready to be a *financial superhero*!

As we depart, I want to express my deepest gratitude to you, dear reader. When I decided to pay it forward and got started with my money resolution project at the end of 2018, to write and self-publish a book, I didn't know if it was possible and didn't know if anyone would care to read it. I never intended to write a second book but people's feedback and comments about their favorite parts humbled me and motivated me to do it again. A year later, I'm incredibly glad I did and hopeful that these hacks resonated with you and will help you in your journey. Of course, if you haven't read "The Money Resolution", head there next! It is also full of money hacks and tons of foundational finance education to help you get good with your money.

Either way, I'd love to stay in touch and hear your stories and feedback. If you want to reach out to me directly, don't hesitate to email me at frankie@themoneyresolution.com. If you enjoyed "Money, You Can Hack It", it would mean the world to me if you left an honest review on Amazon or Good Reads to help other people discover it. It really does make my day to hear from readers in any way, shape, or form.

My journey continues on YouTube. Find and follow "The Money Resolution" there for weekly videos on all things personal finance. If you want to stay updated, sign up for email updates at www.TheMoneyResolution.com and find @TheMoneyResolution on all the social channels. If you post about this book, please include #MYCHIBOOK so I can easily find it and give you a virtual high five.

Best of luck to you on your money journey. Thank you for your time and attention. When financial times feel tough, I hope you always remember: *money, I CAN hack it!*

-Frankie

PS: Reading is the ULTIMATE hack. But you already know that by now!

Don't forget: Claim your "Money, You Can Hack It" bonuses. Go to www.TheMoneyResolution.com/HackIt to get your additional hacks and resources!

Quiz Answers: 1-D, 2-C, 3-C, 4-B, 5-C, 6-C. Want another short money quiz? Less than 3% of Americans can pass the one from GoBankingRates.com, listed last in References.

Acknowledgments

I wish to thank and acknowledge my people and my team: Claire Sander, Rob Walker, Alfonso Dueñas, Nick Rutledge, Steven Malone, Hunter Volk, Jason Sanio, Sarah Elson, Jenn Sahagun, Jim Sander, Pat Bransteitter (hi mom!), Andy Layman, and Kimberly Gonzalez.

You all kick a$$ and your support means the world to me!

About The Author

FRANKIE CALKINS (M. ED.) is a personal finance author and former educator from the Pacific Northwest, on a mission to make learning about money simple, accessible, and fun. His first book, "The Money Resolution" was an Amazon best seller and featured by Teach for America's One Day Magazine, Delta Upsilon Magazine, and The Stacking Benjamin's Show Podcast. He runs a YouTube channel also called The Money Resolution, which has become his main hobby outside of Mario Kart, long walks near the lake with his new puppy Leo, and imagining he's a Seattle Mariner when playing softball. Learn more at www.TheMoneyResolution.com

Resources

For a complete list of all resources referenced in the book, including the downloadable checklist, visit www.TheMoneyResolution.com/HackIt

References

CHAPTER 1
www.thepennyhoarder.com/budgeting/bullet-journal-budget/

CHAPTER 2
news.northwesternmutual.com/planning-and-progress-2018
www.fool.com/retirement/2019/02/16/25-of-americans-expect-to-die-in-debt.aspx

CHAPTER 3
www.forbes.com/sites/zackfriedman/2019/04/18/no-savings-retirement/#7af1c4643d76
www.washingtonpost.com/business/2019/05/31/millennials-have-an-average-net-worth-thats-significantly-less-than-previous-generations/
www.cnbc.com/2017/04/19/38-year-old-retired-millionaire-one-simple-habit-leads-to-wealth.html
www.cnbc.com/2018/03/15/olympian-adam-rippon-heres-how-i-save-money.html
www.forbes.com/sites/zackfriedman/2019/04/18/no-savings-

retirement/#7af1c4643d76
www.cnbc.com/2019/10/18/minimum-amount-of-money-you-need-in-an-emergency-fund.html
www.removetheguesswork.com/author/nickintegritywa-net/

CHAPTER 5
www.globenewswire.com/news-release/2019/10/22/1933510/0/en/New-Hometap-Study-Shows-1-in-5-U-S-Homeowners-Feel-House-Rich-Cash-Poor-and-It-s-Getting-Worse.html
s2.q4cdn.com/437609071/files/doc_news/research/2019/Boomerang-Generation-Returning-to-the-Nest.pdf
www.investopedia.com/articles/pf/07/mcmansion.asp
www.marketwatch.com/story/why-the-american-dream-of-owning-a-big-home-is-way-overrated-in-one-chart-2018-05-21

CHAPTER 6
www.washingtonpost.com/business/2019/05/31/millennials-have-an-average-net-worth-thats-significantly-less-than-previous-generations/
www.fool.com/retirement/2019/01/14/are-you-wasting-5339-a-year-the-average-american-i.aspx
www.cnbc.com/2018/08/20/how-much-millennials-spend-at-restaurants-each-month.html
www.usatoday.com/story/money/business/2017/06/26/study-millennials-spending-eats-up-their-savings/103206984/

CHAPTER 7
www.prnewswire.com/news-releases/average-new-car-prices-up-nearly-4-percent-year-over-year-for-may-2019-according-to-kelley-blue-book-300860710.html
www.eia.gov/todayinenergy/detail.php?id=33232

CHAPTER 8
www.usatoday.com/story/money/2019/05/07/americans-spend-thousands-on-nonessentials/39450207/
www.usatoday.com/story/money/2019/07/30/financial-tips-

millennials-gen-z-who-say-dating-costs-too-much/1855309001/

CHAPTER 9
www.federalreserve.gov/publications/2019-economic-well-being-of-us-households-in-2018-employment.htm

CHAPTER 10
www.kiplinger.com/article/saving/T063-C011-S001-guide-to-state-sales-tax-holidays-2019.html

CHAPTER 11
www.nerdwallet.com/blog/taxes/can-you-take-the-savers-credit/
www.smithsonianmag.com/museumday/museum-day-2020/

CHAPTER 12
https://ahi.org/the-animal-health-industry/
#:~:text=Americans%20spent%20over%20$75.5%20billion,and%20$5,325%20for%20a%20cat.
www.nerdwallet.com/blog/finance/pet-insurance-wallets-best-friend/
jamesclear.com/diderot-effect

CHAPTER 13
www.creditkarma.com/insights/i/fomo-spending-affects-one-in-four-millennials/
www.investopedia.com/terms/1/80-20-rule.asp
www.cnbc.com/2019/06/25/here-is-why-you-should-check-your-market-portfolio-every-day-and-ignore-the-set-it-and-forget-it-financial-lectures.html
https://www.cnbc.com/2017/04/19/38-year-old-retired-millionaire-one-simple-habit-leads-to-wealth.html

CHAPTER 14
seekingalpha.com/article/4329314-turning-panic-income
news.gallup.com/poll/266807/percentage-americans-owns-stock.aspx
thecollegeinvestor.com/1493/order-operations-funding-retirement/

www.investopedia.com/retirement/401k-contribution-limits/
www.irs.gov/retirement-plans/plan-participant-employee/
retirement-topics-401k-and-profit-sharing-plan-contribution-limits
www.investopedia.com/articles/personal-finance/091515/best-
strategies-maximize-your-401k.asp
www.kiplinger.com/article/retirement/T047-C032-S014-already-
contributing-to-your-401k-how-to-optimize.html
robinhood.com/us/en/
www.cnbc.com/2019/10/07/charles-schwab-says-brokers-move-to-
zero-commissions-was-an-ultimate-goal-for-the-firm.html
www.fool.com/the-ascent/buying-stocks/articles/zero-commission-
trading-what-you-need-to-know/
www.moneyunder30.com/prior-year-ira-contributions

CHAPTER 15
www.thepennyhoarder.com/retirement/how-to-become-financially-
independent/
www.mrmoneymustache.com/
www.goodmorningamerica.com/living/story/couple-retired-early-
fire-method-top-tips-66679576
seekingalpha.com/article/4268237-order-of-withdrawals-for-your-
retirement-assets

CHAPTER 16
savingforcollege.com
www.shrm.org/resourcesandtools/hr-topics/benefits/pages/
offering-529-savings-plans-helps-families-avoid-student-debt.aspx
www.gradifi.com/lp/research
www.getpeanutbutter.com/
everfi.com/insights/white-papers/2019-money-matters-report/

CHAPTER 17
www.marketwatch.com/story/more-states-consider-mandatory-
financial-literacy-classes-as-high-school-students-struggle-with-basic-
budgeting-2019-06-19
www.cnbc.com/2019/04/05/personal-finance-courses-help-people-

make-better-borrowing-choices.html
NAPFA.org
newsroom.wf.com/press-release/community-banking-and-small-business/conversations-about-personal-finance-more

CHAPTER 18
www.consumerreports.org/charitable-donations/donor-advised-funds-things-to-know/

CONCLUSION
https://www.gobankingrates.com/money/financial-planning/americans-dont-know-basic-finance-terms/

Checklist

Money, You Can Hack It
Official Book Checklist

My Why: _____

- ☐ 1 Determine your why ^
- ☐ 2 The just one thing rule
- ☐ 3 Create lists
- ☐ 4 Dedicate 5 minutes a day
- ☐ 5 Utilize the weekend
- ☐ 6 Make a 100% decision
- ☐ 7 Start with the end in mind
- ☐ 8 Pay off debts in order
- ☐ 9 Pick a credit card payoff strategy
- ☐ 10 Divert your savings
- ☐ 11 Boost your credit score
- ☐ 12 Create goals and automate
- ☐ 13 Reward yourself, save instead
- ☐ 14 Bank 100% of your windfalls
- ☐ 15 Take a money-saving challenge
- ☐ 16 Double your emergency fund
- ☐ 17 Starve and stack
- ☐ 18 Don't lose sight of your numbers
- ☐ 19 Create a money roadblock
- ☐ 20 Ask yourself: can I afford 5?
- ☐ 21 Calculate cost in hours
- ☐ 22 Factor in depreciation
- ☐ 23 Work from home
- ☐ 24 Repair or fix, don't replace
- ☐ 25 Be willing to trade
- ☐ 26 Learn to ask, sell & barter
- ☐ 27 Rent
- ☐ 28 Find an affordable rental
- ☐ 29 Live with family
- ☐ 30 First-time buyer programs
- ☐ 31 Home buying house hunting hacks
- ☐ 32 Hack your mortgage payments
- ☐ 33 House hacking
- ☐ 34 Go tiny

- ☐ 35 Learn to hack it as a cook
- ☐ 36 Stock up on bevies in bulk
- ☐ 37 Order your groceries online
- ☐ 38 BYO Food
- ☐ 39 Go two-wheelin'
- ☐ 40 Four-wheelin' hacks
- ☐ 41 Find cheap gas
- ☐ 42 Travel hacks
- ☐ 43 Cell phone hacks
- ☐ 44 Dating & relationship hacks
- ☐ 45 Entertainment hacks
- ☐ 46 HSA health care hacks
- ☐ 47 Side hustle online
- ☐ 48 Negotiate your salary
- ☐ 49 Label your credit cards
- ☐ 50 Reduce your taxable income
- ☐ 51 Become a company of one
- ☐ 52 Create a path to passive income
- ☐ 53 Online shopping hacks
- ☐ 54 Use the 30/30 shopping rule
- ☐ 55 Seasonal shopping hacks
- ☐ 56 Use your HSA & FSA on Amazon
- ☐ 57 Join the wholesale club
- ☐ 58 The sales tax holiday
- ☐ 59 Save money with home tech
- ☐ 60 Going out hacks
- ☐ 61 Get a cash back credit card
- ☐ 62 Take advantage of work perks
- ☐ 63 The saver's credit
- ☐ 64 Savings & credit card churning
- ☐ 65 Free & fun hacks
- ☐ 66 Take a money health day
- ☐ 67 Get pet insurance
- ☐ 68 Take a beat and hit pause

- ☐ 69 Avoid the endowment effect
- ☐ 70 Avoid the Diderot effect
- ☐ 71 Mis en place (your money)
- ☐ 72 Learn to say no
- ☐ 73 Use the 80/20 rule
- ☐ 74 Create your 25/5 list
- ☐ 75 Become a closet minimalist
- ☐ 76 Meditate
- ☐ 77 Ditch the budget
- ☐ 78 Tech cleanse
- ☐ 79 Dollar-cost average into the market
- ☐ 80 Invest in the total stock market
- ☐ 81 Invest in an intentional order
- ☐ 82 Get the most out of your 401(k)
- ☐ 83 Trade without commission fees
- ☐ 84 Contribute to last year's IRA
- ☐ 85 Know your F.I. number: 4% rule
- ☐ 86 Adhere to these F.I.R.E. principles
- ☐ 87 Pay fewer taxes
- ☐ 88 Retirement drawdown plan
- ☐ 89 Achieve a F.I. Alternative
- ☐ 90 Set a money resolution
- ☐ 91 Start a 529 plan
- ☐ 92 Student loan payoff hacks
- ☐ 93 Student loan payoff work perk
- ☐ 94 Skip college
- ☐ 95 Find a personal finance mentor
- ☐ 96 Meet with a financial planner
- ☐ 97 Utilize recommended resources
- ☐ 98 Test your knowledge
- ☐ 99 Express gratitude
- ☐ 100 Give
- ☐ 101 Hone your financial superpowers
- ☐ Ask yourself: "How much is enough?"

How much is enough? _____

Created by Frankie Calkins 2020

Made in the USA
Monee, IL
19 February 2021

60815844R00115